THE FRACTURED ELECTORATE

THE FRACTURED ELECTORATE

Political Parties and Social Change
in Southern New England

JOHN KENNETH WHITE

University Press of New England

HANOVER AND LONDON, 1983

Copyright © 1983 by Trustees of Dartmouth College

Printed in the United States of America

LIBRARY OF CONGRESS CATALOGING IN PUBLICATION DATA

White, John Kenneth, 1952–
    The fractured electorate.

    Bibliography: p.
    Includes index.
    1. Political parties—New England.   2. New England—Social conditions.   I. Title.
JK2295.N53W44   1983   324.274   82-40471
ISBN 0-87451-258-1
ISBN 0-87451-260-3 (pbk.)

For My Father

CONTENTS

FOREWORD

In *The Fractured Electorate: Political Parties and Social Change in Southern New England*, John White gives an insightful account of three state party systems—those of Massachusetts, Rhode Island, and Connecticut—in a period of dramatic change. He adds in important ways to our understanding of the new coalitions and partisan arrangements that, in response to the transformed social and political setting, have now decisively replaced the familiar ones bequeathed by the New Deal era.

Political scientists have long recognized that the great variety in political experience of the American states makes possible an abundance of valuable comparative inquiries. John White provides a fine illustration of the research merit inherent in interstate comparisons. The social changes affecting the parties have not occurred evenly across the country. Elements of the new partisan and electoral order have penetrated much further in certain sectors than in others. White's southern New England states prove to be good ground for capturing the uneven effects of contemporary social change on the party systems.

The student of American government and politics needs to know which links between the political and social spheres have the greatest influence on politics and how changes in the larger social environment are reshaping politics, molding it and moving it in new directions. What aspects are the most consequential? We need an "axial principle" that identifies the primary features of American society that together form the distinctive setting for political life.

Sociologist Daniel Bell finds this "axial principle" of contemporary American society in the concept of "postindustrialism." Bell argues that the major source of structural change in the society is "the change in the modes of innovation in the relation of science to technology and in public policy." This change accrues from developments in the character of knowledge: "the exponential growth and branching of science, the rise of a new intellectual technology, the creation of systematic research through R and D budgets, and, as the calyx of all this, the codification of theoretical knowledge." Bell notes that "industrial society is the coordination of machines and men for the production of goods." Postindustrial society, by way of contrast, "is organized around knowledge."[1]

Bell is not alone in attributing distinctive features of contemporary social arrangements in the United States and other advanced countries to developments centering around science, education, and technology. Zbigniew Brzezinski, a political scientist who served as national security adviser to President Jimmy Carter, writes of the emergence of the "technetronic" society: "a society that is shaped culturally, psychologically, socially, and economically by the impact of technology and electronics—particularly in the area of computers and communications."[2] Sociologist Amitai Etzioni argues that "the modern period ended with the radical transformation of the technologies of communication, knowledge and energy that followed the second world war," and that the United States has entered upon a "post-modern" era.[3] Economist Kenneth Boulding refers to the United States as a "technological" or "developed" society whose distinctive characteristic is a consciousness of the "sphere of knowledge" as the premise for social action.[4]

1. Daniel Bell, *The Coming of Post-Industrial Society* (New York: Basic Books, 1973), pp. 20, 44.

2. Zbigniew Brzezinski, *Between Two Ages: America's Role in the Technetronic Era* (New York: Viking Press, 1970), p. 9.

3. Amitai Etzioni, *The Active Society* (New York: The Free Press, 1968), p. vii.

4. Kenneth Boulding, *The Meaning of the Twentieth Century: The Great Transition* (New York: Harper & Row, 1964).

No label can capture to every observer's satisfaction the complex properties of the new social setting. "Postindustrial" is surely no exception to this general rule. But this term has attained wide currency, wider than any other, and it seems to be an acceptable shorthand reference for a bundle of societal developments that are generally recognized to be important and distinguishing. These complex developments, which stand as the backdrop to John White's study of the southern New England party systems, can best be described, I think, as five interrelated components of an emergent postindustrial social setting.

(1) Postindustrial America is a society built upon advanced technology. Technology surely is not a recent phenomenon, but technology built primarily upon abstract and theoretical knowledge is new.

(2) This technology, based upon the elaboration of theoretical knowledge, requires an unprecedented commitment to science and education. And it permits an unprecedentedly large proportion of the populace to engage in intellectual rather than manual labor.

(3) In the postindustrial setting, the occupational makeup of the workforce differs from that of earlier times in American history and from that of most other societies in the 1980s. The white-collar and service sectors grow. "Bureaucracy" becomes the distinctive work setting.

(4) Postindustrial America is an affluent society, one where the increase in national wealth has been so substantial as to move the bulk of the populace beyond active concern with matters of subsistence.

(5) In postindustrial America, the character of social classes and their relationships depart from previous experience. Increased wealth and increased education, together with a new occupational mix, come together to produce new organizations of the social classes and new class interests.

In *The Fractured Electorate*, John White does a most impressive job of showing the ways in which the manifold changes I have just summarized are changing the political parties as institutions and as coalitions within the electorate. I am confident that students of contemporary social change, as well as students of comparative state politics, will find the argument of this volume fresh and compelling.

EVERETT CARLL LADD

November 11, 1982

PREFACE

In the summer of 1980 several national pollsters discovered that if the presidential election were held then, independent candidate John Anderson would capture approximately one-fourth of the nationwide vote. Anderson's strength far exceeded that of third-party presidential candidate Henry Wallace at a comparable period in 1948 and equaled George Wallace's at a similar point in 1968.[1]

These results, however, masked several interesting regional and state variations. A Gallup poll, for example, showed Anderson receiving a remarkable 40 percent of the vote in the New England states, ahead of both Jimmy Carter and Ronald Reagan, but a dismal 8 percent in the eastern south-central states.[2] State surveys revealed a similar difference: in Connecticut, Anderson led both of his major party rivals, garnering 33 percent of the vote; in Missouri he ran a poor third, with only 14 percent.[3] These data indicate the existence of considerable state-by-state diversity that often remains hidden in superficial analyses of most survey data, and in many discussions of the 1980 campaign.

Given the decentralized nature of the American political system, such heterogeneity should come as no surprise. Clinton Rossiter has observed that "the pattern of formal political organization in the United States is pluralized, dispersed, even fractured."[4] Yet many political scientists have ignored regional and state variations, preferring instead to draw broad and sometimes superficial canvases of the national landscape. The late V. O. Key lamented this tendency:

"Students of American politics have concentrated their attention chiefly on the national scene to the neglect of the politics of the states of the Union."[5] Anderson's 1980 independent candidacy is a reminder that American politics is best viewed not on one giant canvas, but on fifty separate ones.

This book traces the rise of a new social and cultural agenda in American politics and the political parties' ways of coping with it in the post-industrial era. The three southern New England states—Massachusetts, Connecticut, and Rhode Island—serve as the laboratory for analysis. Despite their adjacent location, they differ from one another in almost every other respect. Together, they tell a story of major social change and the responses of the two major political parties.

Potsdam, New York
October 1982

ACKNOWLEDGMENTS

So many people have helped me that to list them all would surely tax the reader's patience. Several, however, deserve special recognition. Everett Carll Ladd, Executive Director of the Roper Center and Institute for Social Inquiry at the University of Connecticut, has been an extraordinary mentor for several years. His encouragement has been timely and invaluable, and his scholarship has been an example. The comments and insights of George Goodwin, Jr., of the University of Massachusetts at Boston, I. Ridgway Davis and Morton J. Tenzer of the University of Connecticut, Frank M. Bryan of the University of Vermont, and Norman L. Zucker of the University of Rhode Island have shed light upon several aspects of the New England polity that might otherwise have gone unremarked upon here. I am indebted to all of them. Of those who supplied survey data from both archival and current studies, I am especially grateful to the staff of the Roper Center and Connecticut Poll—in particular, William Gammell, Marilyn Potter, G. Donald Ferree, Jr., and Linda Basilick. Scott Taylor, formerly of the Public Affairs Research Center at Clark University, supplied much of the Massachusetts data. The staffs of the secretaries of state of Connecticut, Massachusetts, and Rhode Island furnished me with valuable election data.

The fifty-six people interviewed during the project—some more than once—afforded me unfailing courtesy, time, and attention throughout the interview sessions, and in all cases their information was enlightening. I am grateful for their exceptional assistance in helping me penetrate the political thicket. The John Morrissey family of Braintree, Massachusetts, provided extraordinary hospitality.

For the financial support without which a project of this magnitude could not have been completed, I am grateful to the Research Foundation and the Institute for Social Inquiry of the University of Connecticut.

Betty G. Seaver's skill in manuscript preparation and careful attention to detail have greatly improved the quality of this book. Rita D. O'Connor typed the manuscript with expert care, patience, and skill.

Finally, I have been richly rewarded by the encouragement and love of my mother, Margaret, and my sister, Janet, throughout this project.

THE FRACTURED ELECTORATE

THE CHANGING TIDES OF AMERICAN POLITICS

In his classic work, Harold Lasswell defined politics as the study of "who gets what, when, and how."[1] Applying Lasswell's definition to the narrower concept of political party, we know what it gets—votes; and when—election time. But the how—constructing a winning coalition—often remains a mystery.

Political scientists, in their efforts to delineate general principles of electoral behavior and apply them to the politics of the moment, sometimes use a metaphor. Samuel Lubell, for example, uses one in which the majority party is the "sun" and the minority party the "moon" revolving around it: "Each time one majority sun sets and a new sun rises, the drama of American politics is transformed. Figuratively and literally a new political era begins. For each new majority party brings its own orbit of conflict, its own peculiar rhythm of ethnic antagonisms, its own economic equilibrium, its own sectional balance."[2] Lubell's metaphor takes into account the importance of social and economic forces in the forming of coalitions but ignores the importance of long-term issues underlying the tensions between the majority and minority coalitions.

A better analogue might be one between politics and the sea. In metaphorical terms, great political-issue agendas, or tides, are influenced by the opposing gravitational pulls of different coalitions of interests. The composition of these agendas changes slowly over time, as do the electoral currents they create. James Russell Lowell probably stated it best: "Truly there is a tide in the affairs of men, but there is no gulf stream setting forever in one direction."[3] In the twentieth-century United States there have been three great tides, each with its own set of interest groups and coalitions: an ethnocultural tide, a tide of changing economic and governmental expectations, and a tide of changing social and cultural values.

The first tide was already well established by the turn of the century. A vast migration, beginning in the 1840s from Ireland and later augmented by refugees from eastern, central, and southern Europe, produced considerable ethnocultural conflict. Reverend Samuel D. Burchard's 1884 characterization of the Democrats as the party of "rum, Romanism, and rebellion" highlighted the tensions already existing between the economically secure, mainly Protestant native-born and the have-not, mainly Catholic, newcomers.[4] The opposing gravitational forces of conflicting Protestant and Catholic concerns took shape in a set of issues that dominated politics through the first thirty years of this century. Immigration policy and prohibition were two of these. During the 1920s Protestants opposed an open-port policy and gave tentative support to the constitutional amendment that forbade the sale of alcohol. Catholics took the opposite position on both issues.

By the 1930s the ethnocultural tide receded, and debate between Protestants and Catholics centered increasingly on the function of government in a period of economic distress. Aside from creating severe economic dislocations, the Great Depression raised expectations about the role of government in improving the lives of its citizens. As before, religious collectivities directed this tide of contending expectations: the have-not Catholics wanted a government-sponsored economic floor; Protestants supported more restrictive government policies for economic recovery and hoped for eventual restoration of the status quo ante.

By the 1960s most people had come to accept government provision of a social and economic safety net. A 1982 Gallup survey found that despite the election of a fiscally conservative president and Congress, most Americans wanted the federal government to maintain or increase spending for a host of social programs, including food stamps, welfare, medical care, and education.[5]

Forty years ago such issues generated intense public debate. Today, however, a new tide is rising, different in both issue content and coalition construction. At the heart of its issue agenda is a challenge to several previously accepted social and cultural norms, such as sexual mores, divorce laws, and the death penalty. For example, a national survey in 1962 showed that only 15 percent of the public favored abortion; by 1980 the figure was 50 percent. Similarly, only 10 percent of the public favored less stringent divorce laws in 1960, compared with 28 percent in 1978.[6] Environmental and other lifestyle issues are also part of the new agenda.

The collectivities influencing the course of the new social and cultural tide are also fundamentally different. They are distinguished not by religion but by occupation. The largest is composed of non-college-educated workers employed in manufacturing jobs, the majority of whom subscribe to traditional social and cultural values: opposition to premarital sex, homosexuality, easier divorce laws; support for reimposition of the death penalty; and a preference for full employment rather than strict environmental standards. A rival and ascendant coalition is that of professionals—college-trained persons whose support of traditional social and cultural values is declining. The opposing gravitational pulls of these two interests guide much of the flow of both the new and long-term issues.

The next two chapters describe the influence of the three major American political tides in southern New England; chapters 3 through 5 chronicle the weakening of the political parties in the region.

1

THE ETHNOCULTURAL AND NEW DEAL TIDES

Although the major political tides have made themselves felt nationwide, their effects have varied regionally. In southern New England, the ethnocultural tide had far greater force than in most of the rest of the country. From 1841 to 1930, an enormous migration across the Atlantic transformed the ethnic composition of Connecticut, Massachusetts, and Rhode Island. The newcomers, most of them Catholics, experienced profound cultural dislocation and in turn created considerable anxieties within the native Yankee community. The issues generated by this influx—U.S. immigration policy, prohibition, and a host of economic concerns—often produced an alignment of Catholics versus Protestants. Until 1928 the opposing gravitational pulls of a ruling collectivity of Protestant standpatters and an alliance of Catholic challengers guided the tide of political issues.

The "Conquest by the Immigrant"

The Irish were the first to arrive. The failure of the potato crop in Ireland and the death from famine of more than a million people prompted more than 750,000 to emigrate to the United States from 1841 to 1850.[1] Most remained in their port of entry and took whatever jobs they could find. By 1850 there were 158,000 foreign-born Irish in southern New England. The 1855 Massachusetts census reported that if the children of foreign-born parents were counted as aliens, then 62 percent of Bostonians were foreigners, most of them Irish; in Lawrence, 72 percent were foreign-born; in Fall River, 60 percent; in Lowell, 54 percent.[2] Counting children of foreign parentage in the same way, the 1865 Rhode Island census reported 44 percent of the population of Providence as foreigners.[3] A person visiting any of the region's cities after a few years' absence found them radically changed in composition. In 1869 Gideon Welles, returning to his native Hartford after eight years in Washington as secretary of the navy, found that city "greatly altered. . . . A new and different people seem to move in the streets. Few, comparatively, are known to me."[4] The traditional Republican Yankee domination of southern New England was being increasingly challenged by a Catholic, mainly Irish, collectivity.

Just as the Irish immigration crested in 1890, a massive wave of migrants began to arrive from central, eastern, and southern Europe, jettisoned by poor soil and overpopulation in their homelands. From 1890 to 1930 more than 15 million people left central, eastern, and southern Europe—roughly the number who had emigrated to the United States from all countries from 1820 to 1890.[5] For these immigrants, too, southern New England was a major entry point. In 1890 Italians in the region numbered slightly under 16,000; by 1920 there were 229,000, a 1400 percent gain. The number of Poles also took a quantum leap, from just over 5,000 in 1890 to 124,000 in 1920. Russian-born immigrants increased thirteenfold, from just over 11,000 in 1890 to 150,000 in 1920. Most of the newcomers settled in the region's cities. By 1930 over 36,000 foreign-born Italians were living in Boston, 9,000 in Hartford, and 19,000 in Providence. Like the Irish, the newer arrivals gravitated toward particular city blocks. "Little Italys" were commonplace—the Federal Hill section of Providence was one. Another Providence district was unofficially named "Jewtown."[6]

By 1920 the transformation from a once-homogeneous enclave to an ethnic polyglot was so complete that one writer spoke of the "conquest of New England by the immigrant."[7] The transformation had not been a smooth one, however. Many greeted the Catholic newcomers with open hostility. In 1854 a Catholic church in Boston was destroyed by gunpowder by Protestant militants. The established, largely Protestant, citizenry bemoaned the creation of "virtual papal states."[8] During the 1850s the Know-Nothing party, an anti-immigrant, anti-Catholic coalition, won impressive victories in southern New England: in 1854 it captured all the Massachusetts statewide offices and did well in the Rhode Island and Connecticut elections, too.[9] Efforts to delay the inevitable included severe restriction of the franchise. In Rhode Island, for example, the Yankee oligarchy until 1888 limited the vote to "native" males, effectively barring 60 percent of the state's population from the polls.[10]

In the 1920s the region's Protestants sought to counteract the threat to their continued dominance by closing the door to future immigrants. Massachusetts Republican Henry Cabot Lodge led the cause in the U.S. Senate. In 1921 Congress limited entry of all nationalities to a yearly quota not to exceed 3 percent of foreign-born persons already living in the United States, as established by the 1910 Census. An even more restrictive measure in 1924 limited the annual quota to 1 percent, based on the number of foreign-born persons living in the United States as determined by the 1890 Census.[11] The *Providence Visitor*, official newspaper of the Catholic diocese of Providence, decried the "fangs" in the new law as "a sop to labor, balm to the prejudiced, and the first practical measure proclaiming an ascendancy of the Anglo-Saxon race."[12]

The resultant Protestant–Catholic tensions created a new issue agenda largely composed of ethnocultural concerns.[13] The platforms of the political parties provided a "stage" upon which the opposing Protestant–Catholic interests could express their contrasting views. For example, the Democrats were more supportive than the Republicans of an unrestricted immigration policy. As early as 1913 Massachusetts Democrats proclaimed themselves "unalterably opposed to any further restriction of immigration," while the state's Republicans adopted a strong anti-immigration plank: "We believe that some system should be devised whereby undesirable aliens should be entirely excluded, and that desirable aliens should be more carefully distributed throughout the country."[14] On the issue of prohibition, Democrats in lower New England sympathized with Catholic objections and called for repeal of the Eighteenth Amendment. The Connecticut platform for 1928 was typical: "The Democratic party calls attention to the fact that Connecticut has never ratified this amendment, and by its enactment and that of the laws to give it effect the citizens of the commonwealth have been deprived of their just right to administer their private affairs."[15] In Rhode Island, the leading newspaper correctly accused that state's Democrats of adopting a "wringing wet" stand.[16]

Democrats also consistently adopted positions designed to improve the economic lot of the foreigners. In 1910 Massachusetts Democrats supported "all progressive labor legislation including the Workingman's Compensation Act . . . shorter hours for women and children, and the Eight-Hour Bill twice defeated by [Republican] Governor Draper."[17] Connecticut Democrats in 1920 advocated "suitable health and social insurance, the eight hour day for women and children and the upward revision of the awards provided under the Workmen's Compensation Act."[18] In 1924 they supported a constitutional amendment against child labor.[19] Such recommendations were notably absent from Republican state platforms of the time, largely because the interests of the Connecticut Yankees lay in preserving the status quo. Thus, on the all-important ethnocultural and economic issues there was a profound difference between the two major parties.

Until 1928, the combined efforts of Protestant Yankee Republicans to retain political dominance were largely successful. Austin Ranney's index of interparty competition for the period 1900–1928 reveals a remarkable degree of homogeneity: all three states qualified as "modified one-party Republican" bastions.[20] The new restrictions, however, could not delay forever the erosion of popular strength.

Having adopted a strategy designed to woo Catholic Americans, the Democratic party served as the instrument by which the Catholics could seize control of the political and governmental institu-

tions. U.S. Senator Edward M. Kennedy notes: "As far back as the
1890s, when my grandfather John F. Fitzgerald ran for Congress, it
would have been unthinkable for him to run as a Republican."[21] In
1913 David I. Walsh became the first Massachusetts governor of
Irish heritage.[22] The Democratic proclivity toward newcomer nominees culminated in 1928.

By 1928, after years of assimilation, the largely Catholic newcomers were ready to exercise a major electoral role. In that year
the Democrats nominated Governor Alfred E. Smith of New York
for president. During his long career Smith personified the eastern,
"wet," urban, and Catholic elements of the party. He was born on
New York City's East Side, the son of an Irish immigrant. This Ro-
man Catholic and onetime fishmarket worker ran for governor five
times, losing only in the Republican landslide of 1920. His presidential nomination was more than a personal triumph; it signified acceptance at last of the group of which he was a member. The *New
Republic* observed, "For the first time a representative of the un-
pedigreed, foreign-born, city-bred, many-tongued recent arrivals
on the American scene has knocked on the door and aspired seriously to the presidency seat in the national council chamber."[23]

Although Smith lost the election in one of the greatest landslides
in U.S. history, in southern New England he far outdistanced his
immediate Democratic predecessors.[24] Generally speaking, it was
the Catholic Americans who made the difference. Irish and Italian
enclaves in the region voted as a bloc for the Democratic nominee.
In sample Irish areas in Boston, Providence, and Hartford, Smith
received 91, 71, and 60 percent of the vote, respectively.[25] Italian
neighborhoods voted for the Democrat in similar numbers: Smith
received 82 percent of the vote in one Italian area of Boston, 79 percent in a Providence district, and 65 percent in a Hartford ward.[26]
These figures are in sharp contrast to Smith's showing in rural,
largely Protestant, areas, where he averaged only 18, 21, and 25
percent of the vote in Massachusetts, Rhode Island, and Connecticut, respectively.[27]

Undoubtedly, ethnocultural concerns largely accounted for Smith's

large majorities in Catholic areas and his significantly poorer showing in rural, Protestant localities. The *Springfield Republican* reported in 1928 that when Massachusetts voters discussed politics,
they talked in "terms of French, Irish, Pole, and Yankee or Catholic
and non-Catholic." The paper concluded, "Votes will undoubtedly
be cast on other issues, particularly prohibition and prosperity, but
when you get down to the ground there's 'dirt'!"[28]

The Catholic voting blocs tipped Massachusetts and Rhode Island
into the Smith column and almost put Connecticut there. This was
only the second time since the founding of the Republican party
that Massachusetts and Rhode Island had gone Democratic; the first
was in 1912, when Theodore Roosevelt's Bull Moose candidacy split
the Republican vote. Catholic solidarity had enormous electoral
benefits for the Democratic party. In Boston, Hartford, and Providence, Smith's reception surpassed not only that of any previous
presidential candidate but also the welcomes extended to the current folk hero, Charles Lindbergh: 750,000 in Boston; 100,000 in
Hartford; 40,000 in Providence. Numbers alone, however, do not
reveal the intensity of feeling in the crowds. According to the *Boston Evening Globe*: "No Boston crowd before ever went so mad. No
other man ever called up such fervent joyous tumult of emotion
from the deep wells of the heart of the city as this best loved son of
American city life."[29] Smith himself later wrote of that reception,
"So intense was the feeling, so large the throng, that at times I
feared for the safety of Mrs. Smith riding with me in the auto-
mobile."[30] The *Hartford Courant* recounted a similar outpouring:
"It was a spontaneous acclamation . . . almost insane in its vehe-
mence and unlike any demonstration ever before seen in this city."[31]
In a prophetic incident during Smith's 1928 Providence visit, city
police tried to remove a flag display, arguing that an ordinance per-
mitted such use only on national holidays. Providence's Catholic
mayor, James Dunne, overruled the police, saying the Smith visit
was of national significance. The flags remained.[32]

The ethnocultural forces that Smith represented had a lasting impact on the region. The propensity of Catholics to identify with the

Democratic party resulted in a competitive two-party environment throughout southern New England. By 1932 the influence of the Catholic vote on the electoral politics of southern New England was becoming evident in the success of the Democratic party. Nowhere was the intense political competition more visible than in the gubernatorial contests. Of the eighteen elections held in Massachusetts and Rhode Island from 1930 through 1964, the Democrats averaged 50 and 53 percent of the vote, respectively; of the fourteen held in Connecticut, they averaged 51 percent.

Franklin Roosevelt's New Deal programs helped to reinforce Catholic Democratic attachments. With only a few disruptions, Catholic Democrats and Protestant Republicans remained loyal to their respective parties.[33] A comparison of the 1928 and 1948 presidential election returns illustrates the persistence of religion as a factor in predicting voting behavior. In Providence the 1948 Democratic percentage in an Italian district was only 3 percent higher than in 1928; a Boston Italian ward, a single percentage point; and a Hartford Italian ward, 12 percent.[34] Irish neighborhoods were much the same. In Boston and Providence, there was a drop of 4 percent, but Hartford's Irish ward registered a 5 percent gain.[35] WASP enclaves in the three state capitals were also consistent. In Beacon Hill the Republican vote declined by a mere percentage point between 1928 and 1948.

The New Deal Tide

The bonds forged between Catholics and Democrats remained so persistent that, according to Rhode Islander John Chafee, "Franklin Roosevelt really should have the biggest monument erected to him by the Democratic party of anybody in its history."[36] But although the contending coalitions in southern New England politics continued to be Protestant and Catholic, the underlying direction of the political tide had fundamentally changed. Older bones of contention, specifically prohibition and immigration policy, were settled. The Eighteenth Amendment was revoked by the Twenty-first, and by 1933 immigration policy was no longer a major issue. New controversies had arisen and were quickly assimilated into the existing Protestant–Catholic fracture. Roosevelt's advocacy of an active role for the federal government in promoting the economic well-being of have-not Americans stirred debate over government's proper functions, both in the national economy and in the lives of its citizens. The controversy lasted almost thirty years, and for the most part Catholics and Protestants continued to align themselves on opposite sides. Protestants, who were generally among the haves, fretted about government interventionism, while Catholics, who were generally among the have-nots, felt they had much to gain from it.

As the new tide advanced, it affected both party organizations and government institutions, especially the state legislatures. As in the 1920s, party platforms acted as a "stage," reflecting the concerns of their respective constituencies and setting the tone for formulation of policy.

The Republican response to the new political tide was considerably more anguished in southern New England than in the nation as a whole. Perceiving their loss of majority-party status, GOP state platform writers insisted that the party was not anti-immigrant; rather, they objected to federal administration of relief and other programs and reasoned generally in the following fashion: "We maintain that such problems as education, the relationship between employee and employer, the case of the unfortunate, and old age pensions, not only are by the Constitution expressly reserved to the states, but in practice cannot be satisfactorily handled by any federal agency far removed from the varying conditions in the several states."[37] That same year, however, Rhode Island's Republican platform described unemployment relief as having "reached proportions beyond the ability of many localities to meet."[38]

The parties' platform rhetoric obliquely acknowledged the shift in the relative positions of the collectivities. The New Deal violated hallowed traditions; most Republicans believed it was prolonging rather than alleviating the depression.[39] In the view of Connecticut formulators, greater personal initiative and a balanced budget could solve the economic difficulties of the have-nots:

We deplore the tendency toward paternalism, and we believe that self-reliance upon the part of the citizen and proper reward for his thrift should be the objects of all law. . . . We are opposed to direct government competition with private business. We do not believe that the domination of an all-wise federal government can ever be a substitute for the liberty of a citizen. . . . We deplore the greatly increased cost of government and the large number of federal bureaus and offices which have been created under the Democratic administration.[40]

Catholics were not interested in partisan dogma but in help for themselves. If breaking such commandments as "Thou shalt balance the budget" and "Thou shalt not transfer power from the states to the federal government" benefited them, why should they condemn their Democratic transgressors?

As Catholic dominance increased, the Democrats began to attain majority status, electing governors and more state legislators. Rhode Island Democrats in 1935 held, for the first time, both the governorship and a majority in the General Assembly.[41] The items ratified in the legislature reflected their concerns: a forty-eight-hour work week for women and minors, mandatory school attendance for children under sixteen, liberalization of workmen's compensation, and extension of a mother's aid program to include foreign-born mothers. The Democrats boasted, "Never in the history of the state was so much legislation beneficial to labor enacted as was placed on the statute books of the state during the legislative sessions of 1935 and 1936," adding, "For generations the Democratic Party in this state was only able to make promises to the people of what it would accomplish if entrusted with power, and on this occasion the party is able to report on the accomplishments made."[42]

As in the 1920s, elective officeholders, particularly Catholic Democrats, mirrored the Protestant–Catholic split. As persons representing major Catholic ethnic groups sought political office, the rallying cry of party leaders was "Balance the ticket!" So firm was the commitment to the so-called eleventh commandment that certain slots came to be reserved for particular ethnic groups. For example, in Connecticut from 1946 to 1962, the Democratic nominee for state treasurer was usually an Italian; in Rhode Island for forty years Franco-Americans represented the First Congressional District and Irishmen the Second.[43] The importance party leaders attached to ethnic considerations extended to running the state government itself. Like certain elective offices, certain government jobs were reserved for persons of one ethnic group or another. Former Rhode Island U.S. Senator John Pastore's promotion early in his political career to be an assistant attorney general is illustrative: "The only reason I went over to the Attorney General's Department was because Mike DeCiantis, who was an assistant attorney general, resigned. . . . In other words . . . they had an Italo-American as an assistant attorney general, and when he got out they had to have another Italo-American."[44]

Eventually the Republican parties decided that they should play the ethnic numbers game, too. Although they had tried sporadically to give some ethnic balance to their tickets, not until the late 1950s and early 1960s did they make it a regular practice. In 1956 Rhode Island Republicans nominated for governor an Italo-American and former Democrat, Christopher DelSesto. DelSesto lost to Irish incumbent Dennis J. Roberts in an infamous "long count,"[45] but won the office in 1958. Ethnic considerations figured prominently in the Republican gubernatorial nomination of Italian John Volpe in 1960 in Massachusetts, where a notoriously weak Democratic organization could not come up with a balanced ticket. This inability to impose party discipline had resulted in "all green," or "all Irish," tickets. Capitalizing on Italian dissatisfaction, the Republicans discovered that there were rewards in pursuing an ethnic strategy.

Ethnic considerations continue to influence party choice somewhat, especially in Rhode Island and Connecticut. In 1946 Rhode Island had its first Italian governor, John O. Pastore, who later was the first Italian to sit in the U.S. Senate. In 1974 Ella T. Grasso became the first candidate of Italian extraction to be elected governor of Connecticut.

An Old Fracture Loses Its Salience

In southern New England today the historic Protestant–Catholic fracture still continues to find expression in terms of party identification. In 1981–1982, only 20 percent of Protestants surveyed in Connecticut expressed support for the Democratic party, compared with 39 percent of Catholics.[46] And in Massachusetts 52 percent of the Protestants said in 1978 they supported or leaned toward the Republicans, while 69 percent of the Catholics indicated pro-Democratic affinities.[47]

But varying party loyalties should not be interpreted to mean that the Protestant–Catholic fracture in southern New England retains the same degree of salience it had from the 1920s through the 1960s. Party identification, once established, often persists even when the motivating factors have disappeared. In New England, this persistence has probably been reinforced by the minority status of the Protestants. According to the National Opinion Research Center, they constitute less than 30 percent of the population, the smallest in any region in the United States.[48] In southern New England the proportion is even smaller. Surrounded by Catholic Democrats, the Protestants have remained loyal Republicans.

Regardless of their different party affiliations, there is considerable evidence of a steady erosion of the Protestant–Catholic alignment in southern New England. In the 1940s and 1950s opposing gravitational pulls generated by these interests derived most of their strength from ethnocultural and economic differences. Today these disparities no longer exist. Since World War II, Catholics throughout the nation have moved from a have-not to a have status. Among Gentile white ethnic groups in the United States today, Irish Catholic families have the highest incomes; next are Italian, German, Polish, and Slavic Catholics. Protestants of British descent are in sixth place, followed by French Catholics and by German and Scandinavian Protestants.[49] Recent survey data in Massachusetts and Connecticut show markedly little income differences between Catholics and Protestants. Twenty-seven percent of the Catholics surveyed in the Bay State in 1978 and 1979 earned more than $20,000 annually; Protestants, 33 percent.[50] In Connecticut the 1979 figures were 38 and 45 percent, respectively.[51] The upward movement of Catholics has resulted in diminished Catholic support for government welfare programs. In a 1979 Massachusetts survey, for example, 50 percent of Protestants and 57 percent of Catholics surveyed believed that less should be spent on welfare.[52] Surveys in Connecticut reveal similar attitudes: 41 percent of Protestants and 35 percent of Catholics believe the government is spending too much on "welfare and care for the poor."[53]

Thus, although differences in the partisan loyalties of the region's Protestants and Catholics remain intact, the Protestant–Catholic fracture no longer identifies politically important socioeconomic and status differences. The ethnocultural division is no longer exacerbated by the passionate rhetoric that once characterized the old political hatreds. Nowhere can this be seen more clearly than in Rhode Island. In 1962 and 1964, WASP John Chafee defeated Italian and Irish Democratic candidates for the governorship. His Yankee heritage and the ethnic backgrounds of his opponents were widely known, yet in this very Catholic state he twice defeated his Catholic Democratic opponents. Chafee's margin of victory in 1964 was particularly impressive—61 to 39 percent—even though his Catholic opponent was running on the same ticket as Lyndon Johnson, who roundly trounced Goldwater in Rhode Island by 81 to 19 percent. In 1976 Chafee was elected to the U.S. Senate, and once again ethnic considerations played almost no role in the campaign. If they had been important, according to Ronald Civins-Mills, former executive director of the Rhode Island Republican State Committee, Chafee would have been easily defeated.[54] Ironically, Rhode Island, the most heavily Catholic state in the nation, is the only New England state with two old-stock Protestant U.S. senators: Claiborne Pell and John Chafee. Pell notes that if ethnic considerations had been important to the voters, "I wouldn't be here."[55]

Former Massachusetts Governor Frank Sargent agrees with Pell. Sargent believes that ethnic voting "has gone out with two-button high shoes."[56] For instance, Endicott Peabody, a Yankee Democrat, bested an Irish Catholic in the 1962 Massachusetts primary and was elected governor; in 1964 black Republican Edward Brooke defeated his Irish Catholic opponent for attorney general; and in 1970 Sargent, an old-stock Yankee, defeated Irish Catholic Kevin White for the governorship. As in Rhode Island, the ethnic backgrounds of the Massachusetts candidates were widely known; yet in each instance a non-Catholic defeated his Catholic opposition with considerable Catholic support. In 1974 Massachusetts Democrats brushed aside ethnic considerations and gave the gubernatorial nod to Michael Dukakis, a Greek American, over Irish Attorney General Robert Quinn. Dukakis claims that if ethnic considerations had been an important factor he would not have been elected.[57] Recent polls also indicate a widespread disregard of candidates' ethnic origins. Among persons of Irish descent surveyed in Massachusetts, only 10 percent said they were "least likely" to vote for a Protestant Yankee for governor; a majority of 55 percent said their vote would depend largely on the candidate's qualifications.[58]

There is also some evidence that members of a given ethnic group are no more likely to vote in greater numbers for a candidate of the same origin. For example, in 1974 an Italo-American received a major party's nomination for mayor for the first time in Providence history. For a generation the Irish had controlled the mayoralty, but now Republican Vincent Cianci was challenging incumbent Democrat Joseph Doorley. The ethnic backgrounds of both candidates were no secret. When the votes were counted, Cianci triumphed by a small margin and became the first Republican mayor in thirty-six years. Analysis of the vote reveals that Doorley defeated Cianci in both the Irish and Italian wards by the same margin: 51 to 49 percent. Only in the more heterogeneous wards did Cianci come out on top: 52 to 48 percent.[59] Thus, when given two attractive candidates, Providence voters set aside ethnic considerations.[60] In Connecticut ethnic considerations also appear to be on the wane. For example, the first Italian governor, Ella Grasso, was challenged in the first Democratic gubernatorial primary by her Irish lieutenant governor,

Robert Killian. The primary campaign was acrimonious, but voter awareness of the ethnic backgrounds of the two candidates did not dictate voting decisions. An NBC News survey the day of the primary showed that 74 percent of those of Italian extraction voted for Grasso, but so did 67 percent of those of Irish heritage.[61]

During the 1970s, political currents in southern New England changed once again as social and cultural issues replaced earlier ethnocultural and economic ones. Abortion, once a matter of moral consensus, became controversial. Previous attitudes toward premarital sex, homosexuality, and divorce also came under serious challenge. In the 1960s, substantial majorities of both Catholics and Protestants surveyed in the area—85 and 76 percent, respectively—believed that abortion should not be permissible if the family did not have enough money to support an expected child. Similarly, a decisive majority in both groups—71 percent of Catholics, 60 percent of Protestants—believed that divorce should be "more difficult" to obtain. During the 1970s support for these positions declined markedly. Only 25 percent of Protestants opposed abortion, and Catholic opposition shrank to 51 percent. With respect to divorce, support for the hard-line position among Protestants is half what it was (29 percent), and among Catholics two-thirds (51 percent).[62]

On the surface there appears to be a substantial difference of opinion between New England Protestants and Catholics on the new social issues. A National Opinion Research Center survey reveals that twice as many Catholics as Protestants believe that premarital sex is "always wrong."[63] Feelings about homosexuality also diverge greatly: 27 percent more New England Catholics than Protestants think it "always wrong." Catholics in the region are evenly split on abortion, whereas Protestants favor legal abortions by a margin of three to one if the woman is married and does not want more children.

Differences over these questions, however, are not evident in the United States as a whole; nationally, Protestants and Catholics express substantially the same viewpoints: 54 percent of all white Protestants and 51 percent of Catholics think that divorce should be "more difficult"; 36 percent of Protestants and 30 percent of Catholics maintain that premarital sex is "always wrong"; 47 percent of Protestants think that a pregnant woman should not be able to obtain a legal abortion if the family has a very low income and cannot afford any more children, and 57 percent of Catholics agree.

The divergence of views between New England Protestants and Catholics on these social and cultural questions reflects a significant difference in educational levels. According to an analysis of National Opinion Research Center results, 47 percent of New England Protestants have had at least one year of college, compared with only 30 percent of Catholics; nationally the figures are 30 percent and 29 percent, respectively. When exposure to college is accounted for, the differences between Protestants and Catholics on all social issues except abortion virtually disappear. Thus, higher education rather than religious upbringing is the *single most crucial factor* in determining opinions on sociocultural issues.

One issue that reflects the declining importance of religious affiliation is abortion. Misconceptions abound in conventional thinking on the subject. Although media commentators tend to lump all Protestants on one side and all Catholics on the other, a substantial minority of Catholics in New England favor abortion, and a number of Protestants oppose it. Insofar as religious beliefs still play a role in influencing attitudes toward abortion, the strength of one's beliefs rather than one's affiliation is the determinant. For example, a recent survey of Massachusetts voters discovered that 78 percent of self-classified "weak" Protestants felt that a pregnant married woman should be able to obtain a legal abortion if she wishes; 70 percent of "weak" Catholics agreed.[64] Strong Protestants and Catholics exhibit larger differences.

The 1978 Massachusetts gubernatorial election effectively dispelled the notion that, if given a clear-cut choice between two candidates on the abortion question, Protestants will vote for the pro-choice candidate and Catholics for the antiabortion one. During this campaign in a predominantly Catholic state, Republican contender Frank Hatch supported the use of state money to help pay for legal abortions if other funding could not be secured. Democrat Edward J. King called such a policy "abhorrent."[65] Seldom does a campaign elicit such outspokenness on a topic so potentially explosive, yet the controversy did *not* become a Protestant–Catholic conflict. Although a statewide survey showed that 54 percent of Catholics and 38 percent of Protestants polled disagreed with Hatch's stand, analysis of the voting results reveals that although 72 percent of Catholics who opposed abortion supported King, an amazing 62 percent of Catholics who advocated state funding for abortion also voted for him. Among Protestants, Hatch attracted 73 percent of the votes from Protestants who favored abortion *and* 55 percent support from Protestants who opposed it.[66] These data suggest that party identification played a greater role than religious differences on the abortion question in influencing the Catholic–Protestant vote. Thus, partisan links remaining from the two earlier political tides appear to explain Protestant–Catholic behavior in this election.[67] As southern New England entered the 1980s, its political currents were rapidly changing. Old ethnocultural differences between Catholics and Protestants disappeared, and the intense partisanship that had characterized relations between the two contending interests faded. Intraethnic feuds within the Catholic coalition abated; even the existence of Protestant and Catholic collectivities was questionable. Although some differences of opinion appeared to persist between Catholics and Protestants on the new social and cultural questions, closer inspection reveals considerably more unity than disunity. The 1978 Massachusetts gubernatorial campaign, which involved extensive debate about the issues on the new political agenda, confirms this trend. The results of that campaign indicate the decline in importance of the old fracture.

Thus, while a tide controlled by Catholic and Protestant interests was going out, a new but equally powerful one appeared to be ascending. The nature of that tide and the new collectivities giving it direction are the subject of the next chapter.

2

THE SOCIAL
AND CULTURAL TIDES

By the end of the 1970s it was clear that new political currents were
building in southern New England. New social and cultural issues—
abortion, sexual relations, the environment, the death penalty—
were being widely debated. During the same decade an economic
revolution of enormous magnitude was underway as modern, sophisticated, high-technology firms were established and subsequently thrived. The revolution occurred not only because of the
availability of considerable investment capital, but also because of
the concentration in southern New England of some of the nation's
most prestigious universities. The fundamental division in the electorate is now based on occupation and educational level rather than
on religion. An ascendant cadre of college-educated professionals
favors social and cultural change, while primarily blue-collar, non-
college-educated workers in the older industries cling to a more traditional morality. These two cohorts are now the region's foremost
collectivities.

The Old Industrial Order

Throughout southern New England's economic history the concentration of technological know-how has been of prime importance. More than any other single factor, Yankee ingenuity has been
the spark igniting economic development.[1]

In the nineteenth century, industrial development occurred first in New England, and particularly vigorously in its southern tier, where accidents of invention occurred with fortuitous regularity. Two early giants on the scene were Samuel Slater of Pawtucket, Rhode Island, and Eli Whitney of New Haven, Connecticut. In 1793 Slater's establishment on the Blackstone River of the first water-powered cotton mill heralded the industrial revolution. Five years later Whitney perfected a gun made with interchangeable parts, a product that in itself was of little consequence, but his method of production was the precursor of the assembly line. Their enterprises typified the strengths of the region—native ingenuity and water power—and made possible an industrial superiority that persisted until the early twentieth century.

The textile industry, for example, thrived for many years in southern New England. As technology advanced and new sources of power were utilized, operations grew less cumbersome and factories were no longer bound to riverbank sites. The innovative, complex machinery, however, needed highly trained engineers, and neither the machinery nor the expertise was readily exportable to other areas. At its peak in 1880, the New England textile industry operated 80 percent of the nation's mills.[2] By the 1890s, manufacturing processes had simplified to the point that women and children could "tend the shop" and new factories could be set up near the source of supply rather than near the source of particular skills. Between 1919 and 1939 New England lost two-thirds of its cotton spindles to the South, development of a rail network hastening the exodus.[3]

The rise and fall of southern New England's textile industry is typical of a recurrent pattern in the region's industrial history since the earliest days of the Republic: initial technological superiority and entrepreneurial capital forms a cement that binds industries to the region. As technology advances, the bond weakens and industry moves elsewhere. According to Warren Johnson, senior treasury officer at New England Life Insurance Company, "New sorts of firms form in New England, they grow up, they get to a mass production phase, and they move out."[4]

By the end of the 1970s the industrial order that had dominated the economy of southern New England was rapidly becoming extinct. In *The Economy of Cities*, Jane Jacobs observes that "By the twentieth century, New England plants were closing up and laying off workers. . . . They brooded upon the reason for this loss: cheaper labor in the South, obsolescence of the old brick factories along the rivers and beside the waterfalls, the decay of Boston's docks, imports from Switzerland and Japan."[5] Since World War II the decline has accelerated.

The industries that have experienced the most severe decay are textiles, jewelry, shoes, leather, and apparel, the so-called immigrant industries. The U.S. Bureau of Labor Statistics reported in 1973 that New England's textile industry had lost 200,000 jobs since 1947, cutting total employment by half.[6] In the boot and shoe industry, regional innovations helped make the production process fully automated, freeing it from dependence on a highly skilled labor force. Faced with competition from less expensive imports, the industry either shut down its plants altogether or moved to other parts of the country. Since 1947, 51,000 jobs have been lost in New England; in Massachusetts alone, 132 firms closed their doors between 1962 and 1973.[7] Altogether, the departure of the textile, shoe, and leather industries from New England since 1947 has resulted in the loss of more than a quarter million jobs.[8] By the end of the 1970s the decay of the old industrial economic order in southern New England was profound.

The immediate difficulty created by the exodus of the immigrant industries was considerable unemployment. Blue-collar workers in the immigrant industries today possess little that is transferable in the labor market. Those who are laid off have few alternatives. The result is what economists call "structural unemployment," a situation attributable to changes in the manufacturing sector rather than to changes in the business cycle. During the 1970s, double-digit unemployment rates led to a "preoccupation" with structural unemployment in southern New England.[9]

Structural unemployment was concentrated in towns that depended on the immigrant industries for their economic well-being. One such town is Fall River, Massachusetts, whose location had fostered a flourishing textile industry. But time and technological advances have stripped the city of most of its textile factories. In his first campaign for Congress in 1924, Joseph W. Martin lamented the textile exodus; fifty years later Congresswoman Margaret Heckler was still blaming the textile industry for the state of affairs in Fall River.[10] In 1981, unemployment in Fall River averaged 9.4 percent, well above the statewide figure of 6.4 percent.[11]

A New Economic Order

While Fall River was having its economic troubles, other southern New England cities had undergone a profoundly positive economic transformation by the end of the 1970s. For the past two decades, innovations in high-technology industries have been largely concentrated in New England. Whereas textiles were synonymous with the region in the first half of the century, the electronics, computer, and bio-tech industries have been the contenders for that status during the second half. These and other high-technology industries have produced a new class of professional workers.

Students of the American economy have used various terms to designate this development: Daniel Bell, for example, speaks of a "post industrial" society; Zbigniew Brzezinski refers to a "technetronic age."[12] But whatever the terminology, the meaning is the same: during the 1970s more and more occupations placed increasing reliance on acquisition of *theoretical knowledge*. Theoretical knowledge is essential to the production processes of the new high-technology industries responsible for the professionalization of southern New England. This movement represents a dramatic shift from the region's past. During the agricultural era the key to production was *land*; in the industrial era, *human labor*; today, it is *trained intelligence*.[13] Wherever one looks it is increasingly clear that the scientific and technological revolution is gaining the upper hand.

Prerequisite for membership in the professional class is a college degree. Higher education fuels the region's economy. In 1940, fewer than 1.5 million persons nationwide were enrolled in institutions of higher learning; by 1977 the number was 11 million.[14] The proportion of college entrants between ages eighteen and twenty-one has also vastly increased, from less than 15 percent in 1940 to 57 percent in 1975—and nearly a third of these earned a degree.[15] Since 1947 the number of doctorates awarded has tripled, and the number of master's and bachelor's degrees awarded has doubled.[16]

The reason for these increased numbers is the prestige and monetary reward that a diploma ensures. Justified or not, today's degree is as necessary as yesterday's union card for an engineer, scientist, social worker, or government employee. The requirements for these occupations differ radically from those for jobs in the older industrial order. A survey of displaced shoe workers in Massachusetts, for example, found that almost 80 percent had not graduated from high school.[17] As the ranks of the new professional class expand, the contrast between the new industries and the older, immigrant industries becomes more striking. For example, in 1940 textile operatives outnumbered the professoriate nineteen to one; by 1970 college professors outnumbered textile operatives 490,000 to 450,000.[18]

Southern New England has followed the national pattern. Since World War II the professional class has burgeoned. For instance, the number of engineers in the tristate area, has increased fivefold since 1940.[19] The computer industry has also mushroomed: today Massachusetts had the largest concentration of minicomputer producers in the United States.[20] The growth of some of these companies, especially in the greater Boston area, has an almost fairy-tale quality. Take the example of Digital Equipment Corporation. In 1957 two young engineers from the Massachusetts Institute of Technology's Lincoln Laboratory saw promise in some electrical circuits they had developed.[21] They set up shop in a Civil War blanket factory on the banks of the Assabet River in Maynard. Today that factory is part of a twenty-two-building headquarters.[22] In 1978 the company employed more than 63,000 people in thirty-eight countries.[23] Digital Equipment is the largest manufacturer of minicomputers in the world, accounting for 40 percent of the market.[24] Its 1982 net revenues exceeded $343 million, and its total operating budget was $3.2 billion.[25] When asked what his greatest problems were during this period of expansion, Kenneth Olsen, Digital's president, is reported to have said, "Finding parking spaces for my employees."[26]

Digital Equipment's growth has had at least one significant off-spring: Data General Company, another minicomputer firm, was founded in 1968 by a group of former Digital Equipment employees. In 1981 total company revenues were $737 million, and net income was $50 million.[27] Illustrating the company's remarkable growth is the fact that an investment of $1,000 in Data General stock in 1971 yielded $11,212 a decade later.[28]

The Academic Link

The southern New England states, especially Massachusetts and Connecticut, have a remarkable concentration of industries employing a large proportion of the professional workforce. In the Boston area alone there are 160 high-technology firms.[29] Only Research Triangle in North Carolina and Silicon Valley near Palo Alto rival southern New England in this regard. Consider the electronics industry: only California and the New York City area have as many firms.[30] The primary reason for this concentration is the presence in southern New England of 182 institutions of higher education including some of the nation's most prestigious universities.[31] According to James M. Howell, senior vice-president of the First National Bank of Boston, "What we have is good, and we have it in spades."[32]

A recent rating of universities by the American professoriate placed Harvard, Yale, and the Massachusetts Institute of Technology among the top ten schools, and in the fields that represent the growing professional workforce, they received high marks: Harvard ranked second in business; MIT, first in engineering; and first and second, respectively, in economics.[33] Another statistic points to the vitality of the academic institutions: approximately 40 percent of all American winners of the Nobel Prize were either educated or are teaching at institutions located in Massachusetts.[34] Ray Stata of the Massachusetts High Technology Council observes, "Fortunately, through some accident of history we happen to have the resources in terms of our educational institutions that are playing into the strengths of the future."[35]

New England's "accident of history" attracts a multitude of young people who want to acquire the theoretical knowledge that today's professional industries require. Digital Equipment's founder, Kenneth H. Olsen, came to MIT to study engineering, as did and do many others. One of these explained, "Of course, if it hadn't been for graduate school at MIT, I wouldn't have come here from Texas in the first place. And that goes for a lot of our staff."[36]

Its outstanding colleges and universities have brought many high-technology companies to southern New England. In a study of employment trends in electronics firms, the U.S. Department of Labor concluded that "cities are more likely to attract the trained personnel need in research and development work, *especially if the cities possess university facilities for the continued education of professional and technical workers*" (emphasis added).[37] Stata agrees:

The linkages between the universities and the high-technology industries are very intensive. And if we look at where high-technology industries are flourishing across the country, in almost every instance they're in close proximity to a major university. In that sense, the university acts as a magnet to attract new talent. . . . And then very often, as in my own case, they . . . come here to get educated *and never go away.* [emphasis added][38]

A report for the Massachusetts Department of Commerce and Economic Development lists the principal attractions of universities for high-technology firms: (1) the availability of top-level professionals for consulting, (2) opportunities for graduate education, (3) recruitment potential, and (4) a pool for part-time work.[39] Thus, the accessibility of a veritable academic powerhouse has been a major factor in the decision of corporate executives to locate in southern New England, particularly in Massachusetts. GTE Laboratories, for example, a research subsidiary of General Telephone and Electronics Corporation, established its headquarters in Waltham in 1972 because Waltham is "near the numerous university and government laboratories in the Greater Boston area."[40] The Polaroid Corporation in Cambridge is another case in point. According to a company spokesman, "[Polaroid] has strong ties to the academic community. It not only uses consultants from Harvard, MIT, and other educational establishments but lends a lot of its talented people to those institutions. There is considerable interplay, and the ties are too strong to be broken."[41]

Universities have thus been an essential factor in the professionalization of southern New England. They provide the talent, facilities, and theoretical knowledge that the new class of workers requires. In essence, academia undergirds the professionalization of the workforce. This close relationship has transformed the institutions of higher learning in southern New England from ivory towers to facilities resembling giant corporations in their style and structure. *Universities are today's new big businesses.* The fact that Yale and MIT are the sixth-largest private employers in Connecticut and Massachusetts demonstrates the existence of an economic base that places a premium on the acquisition of theoretical knowledge.[42]

The universities' possession of extensive research and development facilities is the cement in the bond between academia and the professionals. Only the largest companies can afford substantial research and development staffs; the others rely on outside firms, consultants, and educational institutions. The universities themselves greatly emphasize such research and development. One professor assesses the situation at his school in this manner: "At a place like MIT it simply isn't enough to be a good teacher. To gain the respect of your colleagues, you've got to be doing important work of your own."[43]

A result of industry's need for research and development help is an increase in consulting by professors. The professor-as-consultant is not new. What has changed is the number assuming the role. Former MIT President Howard W. Johnson says that 90 percent of the professors in that university's engineering, business management, and architecture departments have "outside involvements."[44] Often the relationship between academia and corporate professionals is informal, with companies engaging professors personally.

Other companies have made formal arrangements with the institutions themselves. North Adams State College, for example, offers a cooperative program whereby students can earn twelve credits for work performed in the business field. Fitchburg State College has a technical writing program in conjunction with Wang Laboratories, and with the assistance of Raytheon offers a graduate degree in computer science. The Massachusetts college system also has established a formal relationship with the high-technology industries through the Commonwealth Center for High Technology/Education, which, according to Digital Equipment Personnel Director Gene Gross, takes a "marketing view—finding out where the jobs are and how to prepare students for them." The University of Massachusetts and the Massachusetts Office of Economic Affairs have established a "New Alliance" between the high-technology firms and the university; the latter's goal is to raise $5.5 million for up-to-date computers and to double the number of engineering graduates by 1983. Many high-technology firms are also endowing chairs in order to promote research in their primary areas. Analog Devices, for one, will donate $125,000 in the years 1980–1985 for a Career Development Chair in MIT's Department of Electrical Engineering.[45]

MIT has perhaps the most extensive of the formal linkages. The school's Industrial Liaison Program familiarizes its members with the latest techniques and explorations in a number of fields by (1) affording access to professors, researchers, and MIT publications; (2) reviewing current research at MIT; and (3) sponsoring symposia and seminars on shared interests. Director Samuel A. Goldblith describes the program:

The character of MIT research is such that it complements, yet differs from, any one company's research. It is probably more diversified. It may often be a few years further down the road, or more exploratory. It strikes, therefore, an excellent balance with industrial research, which is generally oriented more toward products and services. An easy and convenient channel of communication between the two, therefore, works to their mutual benefit.[46]

Banks also participate in the Industrial Liaison Program. Peter McCormick, president of Bank of New England, feels that the benefits are substantial: "For a commercial bank which might be considering an equity investment in or a loan to a company in a start-up or innovative technology field, the program allows the bank to talk with leading experts in that technological field who are often in the best position to advise about the feasibility of the proposed business."[47]

The clear transfer of power from the older industrial order to the professionals and their promoters, the universities, has changed some attitudes in the business community. Gone is the stereotype of the absent-minded professor musing in his ivory tower. Instead of denigrating academicians, businessmen now accept them as full and legitimate partners. Warren Johnson, a firsthand witness of these events, describes the change:

I can still recall prominent business leaders in New England at forums saying, "We can't have service businesses. The reason we can't have them is that pretty soon we'll be doing nothing but taking in each other's wash." There was no conception of service businesses as a generator of an income for a region or of universities as generators of income—in effect, as exporters to the rest of the nation. That has changed. It has changed very dramatically, but all within the last five to ten years.[48]

The strengthening ties between academia and the professionals have also transformed the professoriate's perceptions of its business counterparts. Two-thirds of the faculty members responding in a nationwide survey evaluated "the private business system" positively; a similar number expressed "a great deal" or "a fair amount of confidence" in "banks and financial institutions." Perceptions of those who manage major companies were generally less favorable, yet the results in this category are also illuminating: two-thirds of the faculty members most closely associated with the professionals—the professors in business and engineering—perceived the managers of major companies favorably, including roughly one-third of professors in the humanities.[49]

Economic Variations

The professionalization of southern New England since World War II has been the region's most significant economic phenomenon. The distribution of the new professional class, however, varies from state to state, with accordingly differential effects on the economies of Massachusetts, Connecticut, and Rhode Island.

Massachusetts: A Bifurcated Economy

In Massachusetts, the profound economic revolution of the past two decades has brought considerable pain. In 1976, for example, the Massachusetts Occupation and Industry Research Department projected that the textile industry would lose 7,000 jobs between 1974 and 1985, in addition to the 6,800 lost between 1970 and 1974.[50] The apparel industry's future was thought to be even more dismal, with the loss of 17,400 jobs in the same period.[51] Ray Stata confirms this outlook: "In areas that are still labor intensive and depend upon unskilled workforces, it is a hopeless cause. There is no way to save them. . . . I think there is going to be a continuing replacement of those industries with ones that provide economic advantage."[52]

Replacing the immigrant industry employees are the new professional workers. Areas of the Bay State where the professional class has been ascendant have been particularly vigorous. The most conspicuous example is Route 128, often called the "golden semicircle," where approximately 1,200 companies are located, some of them leading corporations such as Polaroid, Raytheon, and Xerox.[53] The *Boston Globe* rhapsodized in 1971 that "seemingly overnight, Route 128 changed an area with a sagging mill economy into a dazzling science-based Mecca noted throughout the world."[54]

The divergence between the growth in the new professional industries and the decline of the old ones is striking. Chester Atkins, chairman of the Massachusetts General Court's Ways and Means Committee, expresses the contrast in these terms:

Massachusetts has a bifurcated economy. We have, on the one hand, enormous growth and affluence in the high-technology industry. High-technology industry is the largest employer in this state. On the other hand . . . Massachusetts does not have anything above minimum-wage jobs in the needle trades, the dying leather industries, et cetera. But in the booming high-wage, high-technology industry just the opposite is the case.[55]

The bifurcation is readily apparent. In many of the older industrialized cities, such as Lowell, Lynn, and Fall River, sizable portions of the workforce are still employed in industries dating from the nineteenth century, especially textiles. As these industries leave the state, workers are idled because they lack skills that are transferable to high-technology industries. According to Atkins, "There tends to be tremendous anger and frustration among workers in older industries, since they cannot make the transition into the high-technology sector. What do you do with someone who is fifty-five years old and has been a shoe laster all of his life?"[56]

For Massachusetts in the 1980s, high-technology industry, as Governor Michael Dukakis puts it, is "where we're at."[57] In 1980, 6,000 high-technology jobs in Massachusetts went unfilled.[58] Particularly significant is the growth of the bio-tech industry, which Warren Johnson predicts will be the "next generation of growth." According to Johnson, "The proximity of the bio-tech industry to established academic institutions is absolutely critical. There are affinities that develop between hospital workers and academia. . . . As a result, I think the expansion of the bio-tech industry could continue for years. We are only just beginning to see the development of this sector."[59]

Connecticut: At the Crossroads

In January 1979 Edward J. Stockton, then Connecticut's commissioner of economic development, bluntly declared that the state had reached an "economic crossroads."[60] Joel B. Alvord, president of the Hartford National Bank, agreed, saying that the Connecticut economy is in a metamorphic stage, going from manufacturing and heading toward a "new economic base . . . [built upon] the world of ideas, on the professions, and on personal and business services."[61]

Professional workers have contributed significantly to the state's economic growth. In a 1977 survey of Connecticut's largest private employers, most had members of the new professional class on the payroll. United Technologies Corporation, the largest business enterprise in Connecticut, is in the vanguard of the professionalization of the state's workforce. A worldwide supplier of high-technology products to commercial, industrial, and governmental markets, its subsidiaries include some of the nation's most powerful firms: Pratt and Whitney Aircraft Division, Hamilton Standard, Sikorsky Aircraft, Carrier Corporation, and United Technologies Research Center. In 1979 United Technologies' Connecticut payroll exceeded $1 billion, and back orders totaled $10 billion.[62] Total 1978 sales were $6.2 billion; in that year it pumped more than $1.3 billion into the Connecticut economy in wages, taxes, and purchases.[63]

The United Technologies Research Center epitomizes the professionalization of Connecticut. More than 1,000 scientists, engineers, and support personnel in East Hartford explore such fields as nuclear fusion, solar and wind energy, laser technology, and computer-aided design and manufacture. In 1982, United Technologies planned to spend more than $1.2 billion on research and development. Statewide, 1982 research and development monies were projected to exceed $4 billion; much of this effort is related to military projects, but a significant share was expected to come from the expanding computer industry.[64]

The number of corporate headquarters located in Connecticut has grown rapidly; mostly in Fairfield County. These include seventy large corporations, twenty-two of which are on the Fortune 500 list.[65] The offices are mainly service-oriented centers that direct, consult, and process information for production and sales.[66] Arthur Lumsden, president of the Greater Hartford Chamber of Commerce, asserts flatly that "Connecticut is going to become *the* corporate headquarters state."[67]

Like Massachusetts, Connecticut has experienced structural unemployment problems as workers left behind by departing or moribund older industries seek jobs in an increasingly professional work environment. According to figures for June 1977, only 11,420 people were employed in the textile industry, one-fourth of the number in 1940.[68] The result is a large number of available jobs, but few applicants. Lumsden explains the anomaly: "Our problem is that we really don't need the unskilled. That's why we have jobs going begging and people unemployed."[69]

Nevertheless, the transformation of Connecticut from a primarily manufacturing economy to a high-technology, corporate-headquarters base bodes well for the state. In the 1980s, high-technology industries will be the state's primary targets for recruitment. Edwin Caldwell, vice-president and chief economist at Connecticut Bank and Trust, summarizes the buoyant mood of the state's business community: "Time and tide as well as technology are again on our side, as they were when New England started the Industrial Revolution."[70]

Rhode Island: Blue-collar Territory

The professionalization of the workforce is lagging in Rhode Island. As James Howell puts it, "Rhode Island has been a slow dog on a fast track."[71] At best, professionalization of Rhode Island's workforce is embryonic: 33 percent of all wage and salary employment is manufacturing based, compared with a national average of 24 percent.[72] Former Governor Philip Noel contrasts this with the Massachusetts economic picture: "Rhode Island is a state of limited resources. We have fewer than 1 million people, and a workforce of about 400,000. We don't have the MITs. Providence is nowhere near the business hub that Boston is, with its international airport and financial centers."[73]

The irreversible decline of the textile industry has been a major blow to Rhode Island's economy. In 1960 there were 406 textile firms; in 1977, 224.[71] Textiles had become second to the jewelry industry by the mid-1970s, and even in the jewelry industry employment decreased from 32,900 workers in 1978 to 23,400 in 1981.[75] Of the state's 1,200 jewelry firms, more than half are small shops with fewer than ten employees. Jewelry workers often earn little more than the minimum wage, and many often work illegally at home for far less than the minimum wage. Jewelry employees receive no paid vacations and few medical benefits. Skin rashes and exposure to cancer-causing chemicals are frequent. The *Providence Journal* sums up the industry's dreary outlook: "Jewelry work in Rhode Island is life at the bottom in industrial America. The state's largest industry offers little but the threat of illness and a promise of poverty. . . ."[76]

Rhode Island's dependence on industries that epitomize a bygone era has created severe problems. Governor Garrahy notes, "We have had . . . unemployment problems in Rhode Island for as long as I can remember."[77] Former U.S. Senator John O. Pastore is even more blunt: "People are going to buy bread before they buy rings."[78]

According to Warren Johnson, one of Rhode Island's major problems is its lack of skilled workers.[79] Johnson's observation echoes the recommendations of Project Rhode Island, a commission formed in 1972 to study the state's economy. The commission's report cited the absence of a skilled labor force as a major factor in the state's woes: "The normal pattern of personal development in the past was for young men and women to drop out of school in their mid-teens and go to work in the mills. As a result, Rhode Island's labor force consists of a large number of non–high school graduates who have been working in the mills or in similar forms of manufacturing for years."[80]

Several attempts have been made to implant the seeds of professionalization in Rhode Island. In 1965, for example, State Representative Bernard C. Gladstone (D–Providence) proposed formation of a commission to study the development of a Rhode Island "Route 128."[81] In 1972 Project Rhode Island recommended that the state move decisively to bolster its flagging services sector.[82] Four years later a consulting firm urged special consideration for ten industries, including electronics firms and producers of biological products, medical supplies, and pharmaceuticals.[83]

The urgency of improving the state's economy increased when the Nixon administration closed the Quonset Naval Base in 1973. As Johnson explains: "The Navy pullout did a lot more to kill the economy of the state than the people were willing to admit at the time. . . . [It] caused a lot of them to stop and think."[84] Rhode Island political and business leaders are now manifesting a new willingness to go after new white-collar, high-technology jobs. Georgina MacDonald, vice-president of Fleet Mortgage Company, describes the state's drive for new employers in graphic terms: "Arguing . . . whether business or labor is going to receive a bigger slice of today's economic pie is not going to satisfy our economic meal. We need a second and a third economic pie. Everyone recognizes that. What we need now is the recipe for marketing these new pies."[85]

Despite all the talk about developing a new economic base— especially a high-technology one—there have been few results. Digital Equipment, for example, recently bought land in the state, but eventually decided not to build. The Digital setback dashed many hopes and illustrates just how far Rhode Island has to go, as one recruiter, Erskine White, executive vice-president of Textron, admits: "Rhode Island in its efforts to develop new jobs really has an opportunity to focus on the white-collar jobs, perhaps the administrative, financial, and the transactional kind of jobs as opposed to just setting up a shop with more lathes in it. . . . We have a chance to get our act together. And yet I can't say for sure that we're quite there."[86] Johnson is more pessimistic: "Rhode Island does not have the base from which to spawn new, high-technology industries. I think the state's economy will be reasonably stagnant for the foreseeable future."[87]

Changing Social and Cultural Values

The professionalization of southern New England has created a new political tide equal in strength to the two that so strongly affected the region earlier. The two new major collectivities—the large but declining group of non-college-educated, blue-collar workers, and the ascendant class of college-trained professionals—have also created a new political agenda, one composed largely of social and cultural issues. Conflicts on these issues abound between the two groups. The controversy surrounding abortion is illustrative of the new tensions: the college-educated are far more likely to sanction abortion than are the non-college-trained, by a margin of 70 to 51 percent.[88] Homosexuality, divorce, the death penalty, the legal status of marijuana, and environmental issues also split the two populations. The college-educated cohort is less inclined to condemn homosexuality (43 percent, compared with 27 percent of non-college-educated respondents), is more reluctant to enact stricter divorce procedures (30 versus 46 percent), is far less supportive of the death penalty for persons convicted of murder (59 versus 71 percent), supports the legalization of marijuana (50 to 25 percent), and wants increased spending for improving and protecting the environment (73 percent, compared with 59 percent of the non-college-educated). On these issues, education has become the major determinant of cultural attitudes.

State surveys in Connecticut and Massachusetts also reveal substantial differences on several social and cultural concerns. In Connecticut, the non-college-educated cohort is far more likely than its college-educated counterpart to condemn abortion (65 percent versus 34 percent). The two groups also differ on religious values, the status of women in society, and life-style choices.[89] In Massachusetts, half the non-college-trained group opposes state-funded abortions for women who cannot afford them, compared with one-third of the college-educated group. Cohabitation of unmarried men and women is endorsed by a substantial majority (77 percent) of the college-educated group, compared with a substantially smaller majority of the non-college-educated group (54 percent). Thirty-nine percent of the college-educated oppose capital punishment for persons convicted of murder, compared with 24 percent of the non-college-educated.[90]

Age is often a factor in determining cultural outlook. The young more than the old tend to support legalized abortion and easier divorce procedures. Hence, in Massachusetts half the non-college-educated respondents under forty approve state-funded abortions if women cannot afford them; only 36 percent of their counterparts over forty are favorably inclined to such public expenditure. Similarly, 65 percent of the college-educated respondents under forty approve, compared with 47 percent of those over forty. Regardless of age, however, the proportional differences between the non-college-educated and college-educated groups remain virtually identical.[91]

The new tide has developed so quickly—literally within a single decade—that most politicians and social scientists are still reeling from their attempts to assess its effects. The development of the first two major tides was gradual, spanning several decades, and the religious collectivities of the first tide largely persisted in the second. The new agenda has no antecedents; thus, its impact rivals that of the Catholic migration that began much more than a century ago.

The reasons for the professionals' massive challenge to traditional social and cultural values are unclear. The survey data indicate that one of the most salient characteristics of the professionals is their individualism. Whether it is premarital sex, homosexuality, or another of the host of social and cultural issues, the professionals' attitude eschews the old morality for individualized decision. Daniel Bell describes the new outlook as a feature of the "antinomian self"—that is, the belief that the individual and not an institution is the ultimate source of moral judgment.[92] The professionals appear to subscribe fully to the notion of the antinomian self, whereas the heirs of the old industrial order are much more accepting of traditional values, especially when the values are reinforced by societal institutions like the organized religions. In its report to President Nixon on the causes of the 1970 campus unrest, the Scranton Commission appeared to recognize this phenomenon in its description of a "new youth culture" that rejected "the work ethic, materialism, and conventional social norms and pieties. *Indeed it rejected all institutional disciplines externally imposed upon the individual*, and this set it at odds with much of American society" (emphasis added).[93]

Yet, the antinomian self is only a partial explanation for the differences between the professionals and the blue-collar workers. Education is the single most critical factor in determining opinions on cultural issues; and the higher the level of one's education, the greater the challenge to traditional values is likely to be.

The explanation for these cultural differences probably lies within the education process itself. Academic institutions have always been critical of society. As Joseph Schumpeter once noted, academia revels in criticism, particularly "criticism that stings."[94] Today the "adversary culture" of academia has become a powerful political force, in part simply because there are more academics.[95] In 1971 John Kenneth Galbraith observed that

It was the universities—not the trade unions, not the free-lance intellectuals, nor the press, nor the businessman . . . which led the opposition to the Vietnam War, which forced the retirement of the President, which are forcing the pace of our present withdrawal from Vietnam, which are leading the battle against the great corporations on the issues of pollution, and which at the last Congressional elections retired a score or more of the egregious time-servers, military sycophants and hawks.[96]

One reason the professionals are receptive to different mores is the propensity of the academy to look favorably upon change. This attitude appears to have been transmitted to the professionals. Increasingly, this new class, more than any other group, is responsive to challenges to the old morality.

Another explanation may lie in the constant change that characterizes most professional occupations. Given a context in which half of what a student learns in the sciences is outdated in ten years,[97] a sense of change may carry over into the social structure. Just as yesterday's scientific theories are supplanted by those of today, yesterday's social order recedes and a new and presumably better one takes its place.

The existence of an adversary culture and of challenges to the status quo in the college environment is, in large measure, because of the dynamism of the higher education process. Under the industrial system, the goal of educators was to instill in students a sense of pride and identification with American values. This task took on added urgency with the arrival of the immigrants. A 1920 Massachusetts conference on immigrant education held the educational process responsible for ensuring "that our American institutions may endure. . . . We believe in an Americanization which has for its end the making of good American citizens by developing in the mind of everyone who inhabits American soil an appreciation of the principles and practices of good American citizenship."[98] These goals persist at lower educational levels, but they never took root in the adversary culture of academia. As more people have been exposed to higher education, an increasingly widespread challenge to the traditional value structure has resulted in a highly individualistic perspective on social and cultural questions.

The Political Consequences

One consequence of the new political configuration has been an increase in overall Democratic strength. Blue-collar workers have traditionally identified with the Democratic party, in large measure because of their more recent immigrant heritage and the Democracy's early identification with programs designed to improve their economic lot. The tendency of professionals to vote Democratic is relatively new: in 1948, southern New England academic enclaves overwhelmingly rejected Democratic nominee Truman; by 1972 they endorsed Democratic candidate George McGovern with considerable enthusiasm.[99]

Having largely ignored the Catholic ethnic groups earlier, the GOP has now also forfeited the support of the professionals by articulating a laissez-faire philosophy that most of them view as antiquated. The Republicans' failure to align their policies with the interests of this burgeoning new class is readily apparent in the election results. According to Ranney's index of competitiveness, Rhode Island is now a "modified one-party Democratic" state, and Massachusetts and Connecticut barely retain their two-party status.[100]

State legislative rolls provide further evidence of how much the Democrats have benefited from the existing coalitions: from 1966 to

1980 they controlled an average of 61 percent of legislative seats in Connecticut, 77 percent in Massachusetts, and 79 percent in Rhode Island. In Massachusetts the situation is so desperate for Republicans that they no longer even nominate candidates: in 1980, 112 of the 160 seats in the Massachusetts House, or 70 percent, were uncontested by the GOP. At the gubernatorial level the GOP has had modest success. Short-term issues and personable candidates like John Volpe and Francis Sargent in Massachusetts, John Chafee in Rhode Island, and Thomas Meskill in Connecticut have won elections, sometimes by astonishing margins. But instead of signaling a Republican revival, Volpe, Sargent, Chafee, and Meskill won *personal* rather than partisan victories.

A related consequence of the increase in Democratic strength in southern New England is that a declining number of Republican Yankees and ideologues are left in isolation to argue among themselves. Their own private form of internecine warfare, most of it centering on continued adherence to the traditional Republican philosophy of minimal government involvement, evokes little response among the two major collectivities, who accept government involvement. Thus, Republican issues have minimal salience for most of the region's voters.

The economic changes of the past two decades have brought concomitant political differences in each southern New England state. Three towns exemplify these differences: in Newton, Massachusetts, the professional class is firmly entrenched; East Hartford, Connecticut, is currently in transition from an old industrial economy to a burgeoning professional one; and Central Falls, Rhode Island, remains dominated by the old industrial order. The proportion of people with at least some college education varies accordingly: in Newton, 48 percent; in East Hartford, 28 percent; in Central Falls, 6 percent. Because the rate of professionalization has not been uniform throughout any of the three states, these towns cannot be said to be representative of them. Nevertheless, the political transformations in the three communities are indicative of the economic disruptions of at least the past decade in southern New England.

Newton: The Professional Class Regnant

The economic and political revolutions occurring in Newton in the past two decades are a major story in their own right. Throughout the nineteenth century the community relied on the industries of the old industrial order for economic survival: textiles, paper, silk, lumber, and even snuff. In 1890 the textile factories were the city's largest employer.[101] Immigrants constituted the workforce. During the 1840s the first Irish arrived; in 1860, the first large influx of French Canadians; by 1880, Italians were coming in significant numbers; by 1912 there was a large Jewish settlement.[102]

By 1970 Newton's proximity to Route 128 had brought prosperity. Today its economy is dominated by firms that employ members of the new professional class. Several leading high-technology industries, such as 3M Corporation and TRW, have plants there, as do many smaller firms.[103] Many of the newer industries are located in the old textile mills.

The professionalization of the city has had profound political consequences. As the townspeople have responded more positively to social and cultural change, they have gravitated toward Democratic candidates. This is not a partisan move so much as an endorsement of those who symbolize the social and cultural challenges discussed earlier. Presidential balloting reveals a decided shift from the Republicans. In 1948 Truman received just over one-third of the city's vote; John Kennedy barely carried Newton in 1960. But in 1968 Hubert Humphrey exceeded Kennedy's margin, and in 1972 George McGovern took 60 percent of the city's votes. In fact, McGovern, whose views corresponded to those of the professional class, received more votes than Jimmy Carter in 1976.

Newton's propensity to vote Democratic is evident in other elective offices. At the congressional level the city had a long history of Republican representation, including Christian A. Herter and Joseph W. Martin, Jr. By 1970 the political consequences of the economic revolution were apparent in the election of Father Robert Drinan, a liberal Democrat, with 56 percent of the vote. Drinan's successor, Barney Frank, another liberal Democrat, captured 63 and 74 percent of the city's ballots in 1980 and 1982.

Newton's social and cultural outlook is reflected in the partisan alignments of its voters. In 1964, Democratic registrants nearly equaled Republican identifiers, with 27 and 31 percent, respectively; by 1980 the Democrats held a three-to-one edge. Despite this substantial advantage, similar majorities for Democratic candidates are not automatic. Newton's commitment is to a particular social and cultural outlook, not to a party. If the GOP presents candidates whose social and cultural views closely resemble Newton's, issue compatibility dominates. Thus, in 1978 a Republican gubernatorial candidate whose social and cultural outlook was congenial to that of the professionals defeated by a margin of two to one a Democrat whose views were akin to those of the blue-collar workers.

East Hartford: At the Crossroads

East Hartford is a city in transition from the industrial to the professional era. One company is primarily responsible: Pratt and Whitney Aircraft Division, a subsidiary of United Technologies Corporation.

During the nineteenth century the town had some small industries located along the Connecticut River, including eight powder mills, a woolen factory, two glassworks, a hat factory, carding machine shops, and a few tanneries.[104] The *Connecticut Courant* editorialized in 1819 that "East Hartford with its 3,300 inhabitants is in proportion to its population among the leaders of American Industry."[105] Eventually substantial numbers of immigrants began to arrive, beginning with the Irish in the 1840s. By the turn of the century many Europeans, especially Italians, had settled there. Between 1910 and 1920 the city's population increased 43 percent, and about half was foreign-born.[106]

The eventual professionalization of East Hartford was foreshadowed by the establishment of the Pratt and Whitney Aircraft Division. In 1929 it constructed a $2 million plant on hundreds of acres of tobacco farmland, where it employed 800 workers.[107] Fifty years later the company employed 21,000 people in its East Hartford operation, most of them constructing jet engines.[108] In addition, United Technologies, United Aircraft Research Laboratories, and United Technologies Research Center have 900 professionals at their East Hartford locations.[109]

United Technologies Corporation has catapulted East Hartford to the brink of professionalization. In 1975, 55 percent of all city workers were white collar, 31 percent blue collar, and 9 percent service labor.[110] Only 4,200 persons were employed in the textile and apparel industries.[111]

Economic changes in East Hartford have had political ramifications, though less pronounced than those in Newton. In presidential contests East Hartford has usually remained with the Democrats. Truman, Kennedy, Johnson, and Humphrey all swept the city. McGovern barely carried East Hartford in 1972, an interesting result given McGovern's attraction for the new professional class. Jimmy Carter carried the city in both of his presidential campaigns.

The growing political impact of the city's professional workforce was demonstrated in 1970, when an unusual Democratic primary pitted Joseph Duffey, a U.S. senatorial candidate who espoused the views of the new professional class, against two other candidates whose support came principally from blue-collar workers, Alphonsus Donahue and Edward Marcus. Duffey won 43 percent of the East Hartford vote; Donahue, 33 percent; Marcus, 20 percent. Although Duffey did not win a majority, his share of the vote was significant for someone who represented a challenge to traditional social and cultural values just as the city was entering upon professionalization.

Central Falls: A City with a Forward Look?

On the outskirts of Central Falls a welcoming sign proclaims: "Central Falls—A City with a Forward Look."[112] Though well-intentioned, the message is questionable. Unlike Newton and East Hartford, there are virtually no traces of the new professional class in Central Falls.

Central Falls has not always been outdated. The industrial revolution got its start in the adjoining town of Pawtucket, where Samuel Slater revolutionized the spinning of cotton thread. Its waterfalls on the Blackstone River made Central Falls an ideal location for industry and came to be its most valuable resource. Eight textile mills were operating there in 1825.[113] Many immigrants flocked to Central Falls seeking work. By 1860 there were large numbers of Irish settlers; French Canadians and Europeans soon followed. At the turn of the century half the city's residents were foreign-born.[114] Central Falls was booming. The Rhode Island Historical Preservation Commission observed in 1978 that "the years between 1890 and 1920 were, in many ways, the high-water mark of Central Falls' economic development and community self-esteem."[115]

Today Central Falls is a town in decline. Deteriorating tenement houses dating from its heyday crowd upon its streets. A 1970 newspaper article described it as "an economically unviable community."[116] Employment is now concentrated in two declining industries, textiles and apparel, which together provide jobs for over half the Central Falls labor pool.[117]

Central Falls's labor force is largely unskilled or semiskilled. Only 6 percent of the population has some college exposure; the median schooling completed barely equals one year of high school.[118] The result is considerable structural unemployment as older industries leave. In 1975, at the height of one of the worst recessions since World War II, unemployment reached 14 percent, largely as a consequence of the textile industry's decline.[119]

The continued reliance of Central Falls on the old industrial base means that there has been little political change. If anything, the Democratic party has increased in strength. Kennedy, Johnson, and Humphrey all carried the city by large margins. In 1972, McGovern captured only 51 percent of the Central Falls ballots. Other Democratic candidates fared better: Claiborne Pell received 56 percent of the vote against a popular Republican opponent, John Chafee; the incumbent Democratic congressman easily won reelection with 83 percent of the ballots; and the Democratic candidate for governor received 61 percent. Clearly, McGovern's smaller tallies were largely attributable to his social and cultural views. In contrast, Jimmy Carter carried Central Falls with a large majority in both presidential bids.

Central Falls faces bleak economic prospects. Older industries continue to decline, and few high-technology firms are attracted to it. Partisan ties remain firmly Democratic and are likely to continue so.[120]

In each of the southern New England states, then, the translation of the new political agenda into voting issues has varied according to the relative strengths of the interest-group coalitions and the institutional capacity of the parties to cope with change. In Massachusetts, the Democratic party has been markedly weakened; no mechanism exists for managing professional and blue-collar conflicts. In Connecticut, the Democrats have been able to reduce professional and blue-collar tensions through a number of structural devices, one of which is a challenge primary.[121] In Rhode Island, the professionalization of the workforce is still embryonic, and the persisting consensus on social and cultural matters continues to benefit the Democratic party enormously. The following chapters discuss in detail the effects of the two new major collectivities.

3

THE DIVIDED DEMOCRATS

In the past twenty years, the Democratic party in southern New England has moved from a position of parity with the Republicans to becoming the region's "Everyone party."[1] Today in Massachusetts registered Democrats have a three-to-one advantage over registered Republicans; in Connecticut they outnumber the GOP by 220,000.[2] Recent polling data confirm the Democratic advantage. In Massachusetts, a large majority classify themselves as Democrats or say they lean that way (see table 1 in the appendix); Connecticut data reveal a 5 percent Democratic lead over Republicans (see table 2); in Rhode Island, 54 percent of the voters identify with the Democrats (see table 3). Moreover, Democratic identifiers outnumber the Republicans in every major demographic grouping. Connecticut's late Governor Ella Grasso once observed that the Democrats' electoral coalition is "a good umbrella."[3]

The Democratic trend has given the party a series of electoral triumphs, especially in contests below the gubernatorial level. For instance, Massachusetts Republicans have not had a secretary of the commonwealth since 1946; Rhode Island Republicans have not had a general treasurer since 1938. In the three state legislatures, Democratic dominance is virtually absolute. In the 1981–1982 Rhode Island legislature, Democrats held a 43-to-7 lead over Republicans in the Senate, an 82-to-18 advantage in the House; in the 1981–1982 Massachusetts legislature, Democrats outnumbered Republicans 32 to 7 in the Senate and 128 to 31 in the House. The Republican party has almost ceased to function in the legislatures of these two states. In the 1981–1982 Connecticut General Assembly the GOP was more lively: the Democrats had an 82-to-69 majority in the House and a 23-to-13 edge in the Senate. The Democratic takeover of the legislatures is relatively new. As recently as 1952 the Republicans controlled the Rhode Island Senate and both houses of the Connecticut and Massachusetts legislatures. In 1958 the Democrats made political history by capturing both houses in all three states. After 1958—except for a brief interlude in Connecticut, from 1973 to 1975—the Republican decline gathered momentum, and the party is now seriously threatened or moribund in all three capitols.[4]

Republicans have been more successful at the gubernatorial level. Attractive, well-financed candidates such as John Volpe and Francis Sargent in Massachusetts and John Chafee in Rhode Island have repeatedly demonstrated their ability to withstand the Democratic onslaught. Thus, although Johnson trounced Goldwater in Rhode Island by 81 to 19 percent, Chafee won with a plurality of 87,000 votes—greater than the total state vote for Goldwater. Like Chafee, Volpe won the Massachusetts governorship in 1964, defying the Johnson avalanche. He was reelected to a four-year term in 1966 with 63 percent of the vote. Lieutenant Governor Francis Sargent succeeded him after Volpe left in 1969 to join the Nixon administration. In Connecticut a divided Democratic party helped Republican Thomas Meskill into the governor's chair in 1970.

There are signs that these Republican gubernatorial victories may have been a "last hurrah." None of the three states has had a Republican chief executive since 1970, despite an excellent opportunity in Massachusetts in 1978. In Rhode Island, for example, incumbent Democrat Joseph Garrahy trounced a well-known GOP opponent in 1980 by 74 to 26 percent. One reason for the Democrats' continued electoral success is incumbency. As Connecticut's former Republican State Chairman, Frederick K. Biebel, expressed it, "If you were running in a race and you had the pole position . . . you've got 90 percent of that race won before you get going. And it's the same way with the Democratic party."[5] Former *Hartford Courant* political columnist Jack Zaiman agrees: "We have reached a point in Connecticut history where the Democrats are automatically favored to win a state election. . . ."[6] Such one-party dominance in the region has produced several anomalies, the most outstanding so far being the 1978 candidacy of Howard Phillips for the Democratic U.S. senatorial nomination in Massachusetts.

On the face of it, Phillips's bid was absurd. A lifelong Republican, he joined the Nixon administration and, acting under Nixon's instructions, dismantled the Office of Economic Opportunity. In 1978 he became a registered Democrat and announced his bid for the U.S. Senate. He got little support in the primary, and winner Paul Tsongas went on to defeat Edward Brooke in November. Today Phillips is director of the Conservative Caucus.

Incumbency has reaped other advantages for Democratic candidates, foremost among them considerable financial support. According to Rhode Island's former U.S. Senator John O. Pastore, "If you don't have a good chance of winning . . . contributions will not gravitate towards you. People ordinarily do not want to contribute to a lost cause."[7] Rhode Island GOP State Chairman John A. Holmes, Jr., agrees: "It costs $1 million to run for governor in this state, a two-year position that pays $49,000 per year. When you are the party in power you can raise the necessary funds to keep yourselves in office. And one of the major reasons Republicans do not win elections in Rhode Island is that we do not have the financial wherewithal to get people elected."[8]

Lack of adequate financial support for GOP candidates can help ensure reelection for Democratic officeholders. Connecticut's U.S. Senator Christopher Dodd explains how the process works: "I try to do the very best I can at picking my Republican opponent. The extent to which I am able to raise funds and just do other things has to have a discouraging effect on people who otherwise might get involved. So, in that sense, I am . . . limiting the field somewhat."[9] In his last reelection bid to the House of Representatives before his candidacy for the U.S. Senate in 1980, Dodd raised seven and a half times more money than his Republican opposition and garnered 70 percent of the vote.[10]

Even Democratic candidates who are not incumbents have a tremendous edge. For example, when Massachusetts Congressman James Burke decided to retire, six candidates entered the primary. Winner Brian J. Donnelly had *no Republican opposition* in the subsequent campaign. Such automatic victories are now even more impressive than similar contests in what was formerly the nation's most heavily Democratic bastion, the Old Confederacy.[11] In 1948, Democratic candidates in southern New England received an average total vote of 54 percent, compared with 97 percent in the South. Since then the gap has considerably narrowed, and in 1978 Democratic congressional candidates in the region for the first time edged their fellow Democrats in the Old Confederacy 67 to 63 percent, respectively.[12]

The party's dominance in presidential contests shows a similar regional shift. In 1952, the Old Confederacy occupied the top ten positions in Democratic presidential voting percentages nationwide; in 1956, six of the top ten. John Kennedy's candidacy, however, led the southern New England states to cast disproportionately large percentages for their Catholic "favorite son" in 1960. Of the ten most Democratic states, Rhode Island seized first place, Massachusetts third, and Connecticut fifth.

The demonstration of Democratic strength in southern New England in the 1960 contest is understandable. First, Kennedy was the first major-party presidential candidate from New England since Republican Calvin Coolidge in 1924. Second, in an election in which his Catholicism was a major issue, it is not surprising that Kennedy should have done exceptionally well in a heavily Catholic region. Nevertheless, despite the Kennedy victories in the three states, Nixon also performed well. His creditable showing was attributable in part to the vice-presidential candidacy of former Massachusetts U.S. Senator Henry Cabot Lodge. The Nixon-Lodge ticket gathered 36 percent of the vote in Rhode Island, 40 percent in Kennedy's home state, and 46 percent in Connecticut. Moreover, Nixon carried one of five counties in Rhode Island, five of fourteen in Massachusetts, and three of eight in Connecticut (see table 4 in the appendix). Thus, it was not unreasonable to expect the Republicans to return to a position of parity after 1960. But it was not to be.

In 1964 Johnson obliterated Goldwater in the tristate area, and again Rhode Island was the most Democratic state; Massachusetts, third; and Connecticut, seventh. For the first time, none of the ten most Democratic states was southern.

Although 1964 went exceptionally well for the Democrats in southern New England, 1968 should have been a Republican year. The Democrats were racked by strife and at their national convention split severely over the issue of the Vietnam War. Given his good showing against Kennedy in southern New England in 1960, Republican nominee Nixon could expect to do well there against the Democratic candidate, Hubert Humphrey. The Minnesota Democrat, however, not only matched but exceeded Kennedy's tallies in Rhode Island and Massachusetts, the two most Democratic states in 1968; in Connecticut Humphrey ran somewhat behind Kennedy, but the state was eighth in the country in its Democratic presidential vote. Humphrey's showing is even more impressive when compared with Kennedy's in counties that went to Nixon in 1960 (see table 4). In all five Massachusetts counties that Nixon carried in 1960, the percentages of votes for Humphrey exceeded those for Kennedy. In Washington County, Rhode Island, Humphrey topped the Kennedy vote (48 percent) and carried the county with a 52 percent majority. In Connecticut he equaled Kennedy in Litchfield and Tolland counties but lost ground in Fairfield County. In sum, Humphrey was a notable contender in the region.

The 1972 presidential election in southern New England saw a continuation of the Democratic trend despite the nomination of George McGovern, the party's weakest candidate since 1920. Massachusetts was the only state that McGovern won, but he also fared reasonably well in Rhode Island and Connecticut.

If 1960 signaled an increase in Democratic presidential strength, 1972 showed the persistence of that strength. McGovern surpassed the Kennedy tallies in three of the five Massachusetts counties won by Nixon in 1960. In Connecticut and Rhode Island McGovern fell below the Kennedy scores, but not by margins that could have been expected.

The 1976 election was something of a comeback, however temporary, for the Old Confederacy in Democratic presidential politics.[13] As the first native white southerner to be nominated for the presidency since Zachary Taylor in 1848, Jimmy Carter carried every state of the Old Confederacy except Virginia. Eight of the fourteen states tied for the top ten Democratic percentages were southern or border states, but Massachusetts and Rhode Island were third and sixth, respectively. The absence of Connecticut was due largely to the party's disarray following John Bailey's death and to the weakness of the Carter candidacy.[14] In Massachusetts and Rhode Island, Carter surpassed Kennedy's showing in the counties that Nixon had won in 1960; in Connecticut his vote approximated Humphrey's in 1968.

The 1980 presidential election was the first major setback for southern New England Democrats in two decades. Massachusetts, for example, sided with the Republican nominee for the first time since 1956. Of the southern New England states, only Rhode Island was among the Democratic top ten. In the counties voting Republican in 1960, Carter ran behind his 1976 tallies and those of John Kennedy twenty years earlier.

Carter's poor showing raises the question of whether Democratic party strength is declining in the tristate area. A strong argument can be made that this is not the case. It is clear that John Anderson's candidacy cost Carter a number of votes and undoubtedly deprived him of a victory in Massachusetts. Of the ten states voting most heavily for Anderson, Massachusetts ranked first, Rhode Island third, and Connecticut fifth.[15] Anderson's support was greatest among college-educated voters. A poll just before the election showed Anderson winning 23 percent of the college-educated vote in Connecticut.[16] Election returns in the region's academic communities bear out Anderson's strength among this group: Amherst, Massachusetts (University of Massachusetts), 25 percent of the vote; Cambridge, Massachusetts (Harvard University), 17 percent; Mansfield, Connecticut (University of Connecticut), 22 percent; Providence's Third Representative District (Brown University), 28 percent. Carter held his own in these areas, but Reagan stumbled badly, garnering fewer votes than Nixon in 1960. These results indicate a Democratic downturn, but not a GOP revival.

The Professionals and the Democratic Party

The string of Democratic victories prompts a simple question: how has the party been able to quash most resemblances to two-party competition? Two forces appear to be operative.

The first is a simple one—namely, success breeds success. Because of their demonstrated ability to win, the Democrats never find themselves short of attractive candidates. As Connecticut GOP House Minority Leader R. E. Van Norstrand explains: "Winning is the key to success. With winning come converts. . . . People want to go with a winner. And the Republican party has not been a winner. We have won the governorship only once since 1954. And we have lost control of the legislature every time in recent years except for 1972."[17]

The second factor is a rising cohort of college-educated professionals. Increasingly, college-educated voters are identifying with the Democrats: in Massachusetts 59 percent are Democrats or lean toward the party, compared with only 31 percent for the Republicans; in Connecticut, 26 percent are Democrats, 30 percent Republican; in Rhode Island 49 and 25 percent, respectively.[18]

The changing affiliations of the college-educated are vividly demonstrated in areas where professionalization is strong. For example, in Fairfield County, Connecticut, the professionals have exhibited considerable growth; 29.2 percent of the residents have had at least one year of college, compared with 22.5 percent statewide.[19] Democratic registration has closed a substantial gap of 9 percent in 1964 to come within a percentage point of the Republicans in 1980.

Middlesex County, which includes the Boston suburbs where professionalization of the workforce has reached an unprecedented level, shows an even more marked Democratic trend. Since 1964 the Democrats have made steady gains, and now almost half the voters in the county are registered Democrats, while only 14 percent are Republicans. As in Fairfield County, a substantially higher percentage of residents have had at least one year of college: 29.2 percent, compared with 21.8 percent statewide.[20]

The shift in professionals' partisan loyalties is clear from a comparison of the 1960 and 1972 presidential results. In towns with a population of 10,000 to 50,000 in the 1970 Census, regression analysis indicates that McGovern ran substantially behind Kennedy in those towns having a low percentage of residents with some college exposure. As education levels rose, so did McGovern's percentage of votes over Kennedy's.[21]

In their strong support for liberal Democratic candidates like McGovern, the college-educated professionals differ significantly from the non-college-educated cohort. The differences, at first subtle, have gradually become intertwined with the new social and cultural agenda that is fracturing the region's electorates.

The Vietnam War produced the first evidence of the professional and blue-collar differences: the professionals generally favored a rapid U.S. disengagement from Southeast Asia; the blue-collar workers tended to support the policies of Presidents Johnson and Nixon. As the Vietnam controversy grew, professional and blue-collar conflicts spread to other issues, such as military spending and the environment. One of the earliest campaigns in southern New England to give expression to the differences was that of Joseph Duffey, in the 1970 U.S. Senate race in Connecticut. That year marked not only Connecticut's first challenge primary but also the reelection campaign of a censured U.S. senator seeking vindication. Underlying these events was a major social trend: the professionalization of the Connecticut electorate.

Analysis of the 1970 race must begin with events in 1967, when the U.S. Senate censured Senator Thomas Dodd for allegedly diverting monies from political fundraising to his personal use. Dodd, a two-termer, decided to seek a vote of confidence by declaring his candidacy for reelection. But his censure invited challenge, and there were three potential candidates ready to take him on: Alphonsus Donahue, a wealthy businessman; Edward Marcus, Democratic majority leader in the state senate; and Joseph Duffey, a Congregational minister.

Of the challengers, Duffey best represented the burgeoning professional class in Connecticut. The son of a coal miner, he had a bachelor of arts degree from Marshall University, a doctor of divinity degree from Andover Theological School, a master's degree from Yale Divinity School, and a doctorate from the Hartford Theological Seminary.[22] Duffey was associated with several causes that attracted many professionals. In 1967 he was chairman of the Connecticut Caucus of Democrats, a liberal group interested in policy matters and resembling the amateur clubs described in James Q. Wilson's *The Amateur Democrat*.[23] Duffey headed the Connecticut chapter of Americans for Democratic Action and in June 1969 was elected president of the national organization. Capitalizing upon his appeal to his peers, Duffey strenuously sought their support for the U.S. Senate seat. During the primary campaign he emphasized his opposition to the Vietnam War, his desire to reduce military spending, and his commitment to preserving the environment.

Blue-collar workers looked to the other candidates. Generally more supportive of Nixon's Vietnam policy and unhappy over what Richard Scammon and Ben Wattenberg call the "social issues" (such as crime, pornography, and divergent life styles), this largely non-college-educated cohort gravitated toward Donahue and Marcus.[24] The Marcus slogan, "Tough . . . Very Tough," seemed to relate to their frustrations and anger.[25] Duffey did not fare particularly well with these Democrats. The assessment of one organization Democrat: "Joe Duffey does not appeal to the hard hat."[26]

The differences between the Duffey and Donahue-Marcus supporters went beyond the issues raised during the campaign. Duffey backers, sensing the newness of their cultural challenge, were almost overzealous in their commitment. One Donahue aide complained, "The people who support Joe Duffey are almost fanatically behind him."[27] According to Lanny J. Davis, the Democratic leadership "perceived itself to be threatened by a cultural and ideological perspective which it saw as completely alien to its own."[28]

Given his cultural outlook, Duffey encountered a political stone wall—the state Democratic organization and its chief, John Bailey. For years Bailey had led the party to some of its greatest victories. His political philosophy was simple: go with the winner. To achieve this purpose he meticulously went about constructing the state ticket with a careful view to selecting candidates with diverse ethnic backgrounds. He had learned that this was how elections were won.

After the Dodd censure, Bailey decided that Dodd would not have further party support and set about finding another Irish Catholic candidate. This task became increasingly imperative after Dodd announced that he would run as an independent. Neither Duffey nor Marcus met Bailey's requirements for an acceptable candidate. Duffey, though of Irish descent, was not only a Protestant but an ordained minister. Marcus was Jewish. Donahue, however, neatly filled the Bailey bill. He was an Irish Catholic who could, if necessary, finance a considerable portion of his campaign. Moreover, Donahue was liked by party leaders because he was "noncontroversial."[29] Party leaders' preferences notwithstanding, it took a heroic effort by Bailey to obtain a Donahue endorsement from the state convention. Donahue's endorsement, however, proved to be a hollow victory, for Duffey and Marcus had captured the required 20 percent of convention ballots needed to force a statewide primary. Bailey's dream of party unity through an ethnically balanced ticket was in serious trouble.

The results of the primary show the Duffey attraction for Connecticut's professional class: he came within one percentage point of Donahue in the latter's own home county, Fairfield. In Mansfield, site of the University of Connecticut, Duffey captured an overwhelming 80 percent of the vote. Generally, in areas where education levels were relatively high, Duffey exceeded the combined Donahue and Marcus percentages; where the number of people who had been exposed to a college education was relatively small, Donahue and Marcus made a much stronger showing. Regression analysis confirms the point: in areas where no one had been exposed to a college education, Duffey's vote was 35 percentage points behind the combined Donahue-Marcus vote. As education levels rose, the differences between Duffey and his challengers narrowed, reaching zero in areas containing 18.28 percent of people with at least a year of college education.[30]

The results of the primary demonstrate the minority status of the professionals in 1970. Duffey won 43 percent of the statewide vote, but his rivals together garnered 57 percent. If the Democratic organization had been able to unite behind either of his challengers, Duffey would have been an also-ran. As it was, Duffey won the primary but lost the November election to Republican Lowell Weicker. Weicker was helped by Dodd's independent candidacy, which polled 260,000 votes, the largest number ever given to a third-party candidate in Connecticut. Duffey eventually faded from the Connecticut political scene, but the professionals he attracted to his campaign remained and continued to increase in number.

The Democrats' Cultural Revolution

During the 1970s the Vietnam War lost its centrality in American political life, but other controversial issues arose that pitted the professionals against blue-collar workers—abortion, sexual preferences, and the death penalty, to name a few. This new cleavage has fractured Democratic voters in southern New England. In Massachusetts, for example, half of all non-college-educated Democrats oppose the use of state funds to pay for abortions, compared with 28 percent of college-educated Democrats. Similarly, a substantial majority (60 percent) of non-college-educated Democrats favor the death penalty for persons convicted of first-degree murder; a minority (42 percent) of college-educated Democrats do so. College-educated Democrats are much more likely than their non-college-educated counterparts to oppose expansion of the state highway system (61 and 35 percent, respectively). Crime evokes similar discord: most non-college-educated Democrats (56 percent) favor more spending for crime control and prevention; 36 percent of the college-educated do so.[31]

Connecticut Democrats evince similar disagreement on most of these social and cultural issues. For example, most non-college-educated Democrats (56 percent) oppose government-funded abortion, compared with only 27 percent of college-educated Democrats. And to a question that strikes at the heart of the cultural differences, most college-educated Democrats (64 percent) answered that "doing the things that give you personal satisfaction and pleasure" is more important than "working hard and doing what is expected of you," compared with 48 percent of the non-college-educated.[32]

These data indicate that social and cultural issues have split the Democrats into two distinct groups with contrasting and often hostile world views: the college-educated, including most of the region's professionals; and the non-college-educated, including workers in the older industries. When these divisive issues are injected into a political campaign, cultural warfare becomes a very real possibility. Such was the case in the 1978 Democratic gubernatorial primary in Massachusetts.

At the beginning of 1978, Governor Michael Dukakis appeared to be as assured of reelection as had any other Massachusetts governor in recent years. A March poll showed that 56 percent of respondents rated his performance as either "excellent" or "good."[33] Even the weather worked in his favor: a February blizzard had paralyzed most of the state, and television news coverage of the governor in a sweater, seemingly in command of the situation, struck a responsive chord with the electorate. The pundits and Dukakis alike were almost certain that he would win a second term.

The outlook was accordingly bleak for Dukakis's two probable challengers, Port Authority Director Edward J. King and Cambridge Councilwoman Barbara Ackermann. A February poll projected Dukakis to win 64 percent of the vote to King's 11 percent and Ackermann's 3 percent, with 22 percent undecided.[34] Commenting on the governor's lead, King's pollster noted that "it would be harder to beat Dukakis in a primary than it would be to defeat the Republicans in the general election next November."[35]

About this time the King organization sponsored a survey focusing on those who favored Dukakis's reelection: 42 percent said that under no circumstances could they support a candidate who opposed minimum jail sentences for violent crimes; 36 percent said they could not support a candidate who opposed the death penalty; and 60 percent said they could not support a candidate who favored abortion. According to George Frattaroli, King's campaign manager, "That's when we discovered we could get significant defections from Dukakis if we could let people know where he stood and where we stood on the issues."[36]

King wasted no time letting the voters know where he stood. In television, radio, and newspaper advertisements he hammered at the Dukakis positions on abortion, Proposition 13, the death penalty, mandatory jail sentences, and the drinking age. Over and over again he stressed that there was "a clear choice." In a statewide television debate on the eve of the primary, a visibly angry King summarized his positions:

Clearly I stand once again for a Proposition 13 for Massachusetts. . . . I'm for capital punishment versus premeditated felony murders, which are on the rise in this state. I'm for mandatory jail sentences for drug pushers, clear and simple. I'm for mandatory jail sentences for those who break and enter into our homes in the nighttime. Clearly jail is the place for them. I'm unalterably opposed to taxpayer funds being used for abortion. I think the practice is abhorrent. And I'm for raising the drinking age to twenty-one. . . . Those are my positions. Ask Dukakis his.[37]

Placed on the defensive, Dukakis responded to the litany by stating his "fundamentally different views." For example, during his first year as governor, he had vetoed a strong death penalty bill passed by the Massachusetts General Court; the state Senate subsequently sustained his veto by a narrow one-vote margin.[38] During the campaign Dukakis reiterated his opposition to capital punishment, declaring: "I do not believe that capital punishment is an essential or even a valuable tool in the fight against crime."[39] He also disagreed with King on the issue of abortion. As governor, he had vetoed appropriation measures that would eliminate state-funded abortions for the economically disadvantaged. Whereas King favored setting the legal drinking age at twenty-one, Dukakis preferred to let the requirement stand at age eighteen; during his administration, he had twice vetoed legislation to raise the drinking age. Finally, Dukakis disagreed with King on the wisdom of a Proposition 13-like measure for Massachusetts. He maintained that such a massive tax cut simply was not feasible. (In a referendum two years later, voters adopted their own version of Proposition 13 by a two-to-one margin.)

Non-college-educated, blue-collar workers disagreed with Dukakis's positions on these issues. One blue-collar union leader in his endorsement of King reflected their bitterness: "The way I see it, it's us versus them. The liberal intelligentsia, the refugees of academia who have been manipulating our lives with the bureaucracy are now on the defensive and that's the way we like it."[40]

Exploiting their anger, King reminded blue-collar workers of Dukakis's positions on the controversial social and cultural issues. As King later stated in a 1982 interview: "The theme of my 1978 campaign for governor was 'a clear choice.' It was a clear choice on practically every major issue. Mandatory jail sentences for drug pushers, abortion, capital punishment, and raising the drinking age are emotional issues. And the feelings of the voters on these questions run quite high."[41] Dukakis agreed, noting, "I allowed Ed King to set the agenda in 1978."[42]

The primary campaign between King and Dukakis pitted two relatively new but decidedly antagonistic social and cultural world views against each other. Analysis of information on those who participated shows that only 41 percent of college graduates or those who had completed some graduate work supported King; 59 percent supported Dukakis.[43] Voters shared the cultural and social predilections of their favored candidate on an important environmental issue like the extension of the Massachusetts highway system: 53 percent of Dukakis partisans were opposed, compared with 40 percent of King partisans. Only 25 percent of Dukakis supporters opposed the use of state funds for abortions, in contrast to 62 percent of King supporters. Similarly, 45 percent of those for Dukakis opposed a Proposition 13 in Massachusetts, compared with 26 percent of King voters. For persons convicted of first-degree murder, 48 percent of Dukakis voters and 73 percent of King supporters favored the death penalty. On each question, then, differences between the King and Dukakis voters were almost exactly the same as those measured between the college-educated and non-college-educated segments of the electorate.[44]

The primary returns gave King 51 percent of the vote, Dukakis 42 percent, and Ackermann 7 percent. The results stunned political observers. A governor who had seemed invulnerable at the beginning of the year had been bested by a political newcomer in September. Calling his defeat a "strange and wondrous thing," Dukakis attributed it to his inattention to the campaign: "If you have a state which tends to be dominated by one party . . . you've got to put a very heavy emphasis on the primary and not spend too much time being concerned about the final election except in a general way until you get through that primary."[45] King was understandably elated, and in a fist-waving victory speech declared he would not moderate his positions.

David B. Wilson, political columnist for the *Boston Globe*, wrote that King's triumph represented "a counterrevolution against the technocratic, New Class of which Dukakis is the most conspicuous example."[46] The primary figures confirm this claim. In the cities along and near Route 128, where professionalism has gained considerable momentum, Dukakis ran well. Newton, for example, gave him and King 58 and 35 percent, respectively; Lexington and Concord, 62 and 31 percent; Wellesley, 54 and 40 percent. In Cambridge, Dukakis gathered 48 percent, King 37 percent, and Ackermann 15 percent. In contrast, King performed best in towns with vestiges of nineteenth-century industrialism. Boston, for example, gave King 54 percent of its vote, Dukakis only 39 percent; Fall River, 53 and 37 percent; New Bedford, 50 and 39 percent; and Lowell, 50 and 46 percent, respectively. So it went throughout the state—Dukakis doing well where the college-educated professional class forms the bulk of the electorate, and King deriving his strength from the non-college-educated, blue-collar workers.

The King victory should not be interpreted as a sign that the blue-collar industrial workforce is on the rise in Massachusetts. Quite the contrary; industries employing members of the new professional class continue to outpace those of the industrial era. According to Dukakis, "As time goes on, the Democrats who will do well and are elected to office in the state will tend to be more out of a liberal, New Frontier, post-Kennedy generation than they will be out of Ed King's philosophical tree."[47] If Ackermann had not been a candidate, most of her support would probably have gone to Dukakis, and the outcome would have better reflected the essential electoral split.

Under Massachusetts law unaffiliated voters may vote in either party primary, and party members may switch affiliation. In 1978 many unaffiliated voters and some pro-Dukakis Democrats were lured into the Republican primary contest for the U.S. Senate, where incumbent Edward Brooke faced a conservative challenge for nomination. The number of votes cast in the Republican senatorial primary in Boston, for example, was three times as large as that cast in a hotly contested Republican gubernatorial race four years earlier. Presumably many of the Democrats who voted for Brooke would have voted for Dukakis in the Democratic runoff. But *both* Brooke and Ackermann were on the ballot, and the King victory turned Massachusetts politics on its head.

In the general campaign many Democrats, led by Beacon Hill's then state legislator Barney Frank, refused to support King and endorsed the Republican gubernatorial candidate, Frank Hatch, whose positions were closer to those of Dukakis. King's running mate, Thomas P. O'Neill III—son of U.S. House Speaker Thomas P. "Tip" O'Neill, Jr.—did not endorse King directly, saying only that he "endorsed the ticket . . . [which is] as diverse and varied as our electorate."[48] Some prominent Republicans, however, backed King. Governor Meldrim Thomson of New Hampshire said that if he lived in Massachusetts he would vote for King. So, too, did William Loeb, disputatious publisher of the *Manchester* (N.H.) *Union-Leader*. Confusing matters even more, Edward F. King, the loser in the Republican gubernatorial primary, endorsed Democrat Edward J. King. And "Mr. Proposition 13" chimed in with a television commercial: "If Ed King cannot do it in Massachusetts, my name is not Howard Jarvis."[49] Dukakis remained silent.

In November, King came out on top—the only candidate in this century to become governor of the state in a first try for elective office.

Party Structure and the Management of the Social and Cultural Agenda

Although the electorate in southern New England is badly fractured along social and cultural lines, several factors prevent expression of the conflict in the electoral arena. Foremost among them is the organizational structure of the political parties.

One of the major goals of any political organization is to translate society's political agenda into a platform agreed upon by its nominees. To achieve this fundamental task, requires managing intraparty conflicts through internal discipline. For years the Massachusetts Democratic party has been unable and unwilling to impose this discipline.

One long-time observer of Massachusetts politics, U.S. House Speaker "Tip" O'Neill comments:

There has never been a strong party organization in Massachusetts . . .
The party organization fell apart when the Kennedys created their own
party committees. Every community had its own Kennedy party secretary.
The Kennedys were in competition with the regular party organization, and
they were the prototype for the future. Today everyone is out for themselves. When I run for reelection, for example, I put my own group together. We call our friends. We run our own campaign.[50]

Massachusetts Director of Elections Marcia Molay notes that any
attempt to tighten the primary requirements is almost impossible
because "no candidate wants to limit his or her options."[51] The result,
according to U.S. Senator Paul Tsongas, is "a party of fiefdoms."[52]

Operating within their "free-market" climate, Massachusetts
Democrats have not avoided divisive party primaries. During the
1970s every gubernatorial election was preceded by a Democratic
primary fight. No set of Democratic party leaders has been able to
obtain consensus on a candidate and make the choice stick. This ba-
zaarlike atmosphere allowed the King–Dukakis duel to happen. According to Democratic State Chairman Chester Atkins, a stronger
party organization would prevent a King from getting to a forum:
"King is a rank amateur politically, and a strong party has the ability
to distinguish between the amateurs and the professionals in ways
the primaries cannot. Often in a primary it is an advantage to be an
amateur."[53]

Connecticut Democrats have been more fortunate than their
Massachusetts counterparts. There, a nationally recognized strong
party organization has managed to avoid the internal hemorrhaging
so commonplace next door. Since 1955 the Democrats have held
only one primary contest for governor, in contrast with nine in Massachusetts. A large share of the credit for this belongs to one man,
the late Democratic State Chairman John Bailey.

Bailey assumed the chairmanship of the Democratic party in
Connecticut in 1946, and until his death in April 1975 he wielded
considerable influence in the party's selection of candidates. Much
of his power derived from his unique ability to achieve consensus
within the leadership. According to former Governor John Demp-

sey, the key to Bailey's success was his ability to listen to others.[54] One of his admirers, former U.S. Senator Abraham Ribicoff, called Bailey "the savviest, brightest, and most sensitive politician I have ever known. He was an organizational genius."[55]

During Bailey's tenure as chairman the Democrats became the dominant party in Connecticut, partly because Bailey knew how to head off disruptions within the organization. Connecticut law reinforced his talents for conflict management. Under the so-called challenge primary statute, a contender must obtain 20 percent of the votes at the state convention and secure 5,000 valid signatures of voters registered with his party in order to qualify for a primary. Until 1982 in Massachusetts, a candidate had only to secure 10,000 signatures in order to mount a primary challenge.[56]

Thus, although Democrats in both Massachusetts and Connecticut have been faced with the same social and cultural issues accompanying the expansion of the professional class, Connecticut Democrats have largely succeeded in containing the resulting divisiveness. Only once, in Duffey's senatorial challenge in 1970, did this agenda elude the grasp of the party managers.

The King–Dukakis contest in Massachusetts gave Connecticut Democrats a new appreciation of their faculty for avoiding internecine battles. All recent efforts to change the requirements of Connecticut's primary statute, the latest spearheaded by the late Governor Grasso, have met with rejection. As U.S. Senator Christopher Dodd sees it:

I think a lot of us, myself included, are becoming much more respectful of our byzantine political process in Connecticut. . . . We are able to minimize the effect of someone like Governor King or someone out on the left from getting to a forum. If they're really that far out, the likelihood of getting the 20 percent of the convention ballots is going to be small enough so that we can discourage that kind of race.[57]

Unlike Massachusetts and Connecticut, Rhode Island had experienced no significant intraparty strife in connection with the new social and cultural tide. This difference stems in large measure from the lack of a substantial number of professionals in the state. Of the states with the highest percentage of the workforce employed in blue-collar occupations, Rhode Island ranks sixth; in contrast, Massachusetts and Connecticut rank sixth and seventh, respectively, in the percentages of those employed in white-collar occupations.[58] Thus, because its professionalization is only embryonic, Rhode Island remains a "consensus state": blue-collar workers and state party leaders agree on most social and cultural questions.

For example, although George McGovern won Rhode Island's presidential primary in 1972, his victory was mainly the result of a split in the blue-collar vote among Hubert Humphrey, Edmund Muskie, and George Wallace and of general voter apathy: McGovern received 41 percent of the ballots; Humphrey, Muskie, and Wallace together, 56 percent; fewer than one in ten voters went to the polls. As the campaign progressed, McGovern's reception by state party leaders changed from cool to openly hostile. On the eve of the November balloting, then State Chairman Lawrence P. McGarry expressed the opinion of most: "I am enthusiastic about our state and congressional ticket. . . . [But] how can I honestly say we've got a great guy at the head of that ticket?"[59] When asked whether he would vote for McGovern, McGarry referred to the secrecy of the ballot.

Democratic state officeholders have reflected the wishes of their blue-collar—not necessarily Catholic—constituents, particularly in regard to abortion. In 1974 the General Assembly passed a resolution urging submission to the states of an amendment to the U.S. Constitution to "ensure the right to life of every American from conception until death."[60] The 1976 Rhode Island Democratic platform, in defiance of the position taken by the national party, adopted a plank supporting an antiabortion amendment to the Constitution. According to Governor Garrahy, the party leadership was "overwhelmingly in agreement" on the abortion issue.[61]

Thus, Rhode Island Democratic leaders have achieved substantial internal agreement on the new social and cultural agenda. Discussion often focuses instead on economic issues—a carry-over from the New Deal era. According to Garrahy, "By far, the majority voice and focus of the Democratic party in this state is placed on the traditional [economic] issues that the Democrats are normally identified with."[62]

This does not mean that Rhode Island Democrats have experienced no internal strife. In recent years there has been a plethora of primaries as the result of a statute that makes it relatively easy to challenge the party's nominee.[63] In 1980, for example, there were Democratic primaries in one-fourth of the General Assembly districts. Former Congressman Edward P. Beard says that most of these contests involve a candidate's desire for promotion by the party to higher office.[64] As such, they are a corollary of the overwhelming strength of the Democratic party, not of a fracturing over social and cultural issues.

An "Everyone Party" Means Issueless Campaigns

The inclusive nature of the Democratic party in southern New England often inhibits the translation of social conflict into a voting issue; the result is issueless campaigns. Voters attempt to choose between a Democratic candidate whose positions on the social issues are often obscure and a usually unviable Republican alternative, when such an alternative exists. Such campaigns are particularly widespread for seats in the state legislatures, where Republican opposition collapsed during the 1970s.

The trend reinforces an incumbent's natural inclination to avoid potential controversy over the social and cultural agenda. According to former Governor Noel, the issues in this new agenda are "no-winners . . . the trouble issues for politicians":

A lot of your cute politicians try to walk the line on the social issues. But you really can't walk the line on issues like the death penalty and abortion. If you really sit down and think about it, you're either for abortion or against abortion. There is no middle of the road. And it's the same with the death penalty. If your priority is to survive in office, then you should avoid these issues.[65]

Massachusetts Democratic House Whip John E. Murphy, Jr., agrees: "If these social and cultural issues, such as abortion, were brought up in my legislative race, I would try to minimize their impact."[66]

Rather than exacerbate the fracture between the professional and blue-collar workforces, candidates often prefer to stress those issues upon which the two groups can agree. The principal arena of consensus is economic concerns. Dukakis says, "We've always had a split in the party where we agreed on the basic New Deal–Fair Deal economic lunch-bucket issues but disagreed on abortion, capital punishment, and some of the social issues."[67]

Even when confronted directly with a social and cultural challenge, it is not a foregone conclusion that an incumbent will respond to it. An example was a 1976 primary contest involving U.S. Senator Edward Kennedy. In office since 1963, Kennedy had taken positions on abortion and busing that were unpopular with his blue-collar constituency. This first challenge to his nomination came from opponents who, like Edward King, were relative unknowns statewide and who contrasted Kennedy's positions on social and cultural issues with their own. Unlike Dukakis, however, Kennedy ignored their criticism; instead, he reiterated his commitment to national health insurance and to dealing with unemployment—positions that evoked little discord among either college-educated or non-college-educated Democrats. This strategy diffused most of the blue-collar sentiment against him. When the votes were counted, Kennedy won 74 percent, and Boston—which had been riven by racial violence—gave him 55 percent.

In his challenge to Carter's renomination in 1980, Kennedy adopted the same strategy. During the primary campaign, he emphasized his commitment to fight inflation by imposition of wage and price controls, a position that had considerable national support. Of those voting for him in the primary, 55 percent named inflation as the country's most important problem, compared with 25 percent of those supporting Carter.[68] Kennedy won 67 percent of the Massachusetts vote to Carter's 30 percent, running well in areas where professionals predominate: Newton gave him 73 percent and Carter 24 percent; the Cambridge split was 68 and 27 percent, respectively; that in Amherst, 59 and 34 percent. Kennedy scored equally well in blue-collar areas: Lowell gave him 73 percent and Carter 24 percent; and Lynn—whose favorite-son speaker of the Massachusetts House of Representatives had endorsed Carter—72 percent, with only 25 percent voting for Carter. Fall River and New Bedford gave Kennedy massive pluralities of 78 and 81 percent, respectively. Boston voters also favored Kennedy, but those in South Boston may have been influenced by Kennedy's stands on abortion and busing; there, Carter won 50 percent of the vote, Kennedy 45 percent. Given South Boston's traditional association with the Kennedy family, his poorer showing there is significant.[69]

Still, the Kennedy strategy provides a lesson for Democratic incumbents: avoid discussing the social and cultural agenda, and concentrate on the areas of professional and blue-collar agreement. Such a prescription confines conflict to the inner sanctums of government—namely, executive chambers, legislatures, and the judiciary. This is particularly so as public policy increasingly impinges on the fundamental split between professionals and blue-collar workers. Only when voter frustration increases, party leaders are unable to ameliorate that frustration, and candidates adopt opposing social and cultural views does the new agenda become visible. From time to time such a set of circumstances does occur, as the Duffey and King challenges demonstrate. For the most part, though, the new social and cultural agenda is like a powder keg: left alone it is harmless; only in the presence of a lighted match does it become dangerous.

4

THE UNRAVELING OF THE REPUBLICAN PARTY

Wanted: A Willing Republican Living in the Eighth Bristol District with a Strong Belief in the Return of Two-Party Government.

So ran a 1978 advertisement in the *Fall River Herald News*.[1] The objective: to find a Republican candidate for a seat in the Massachusetts legislature. The result: failure. This lack of Republican candidates is an increasingly familiar phenomenon in southern New England. During the 1970s the Republican party declined from a full-fledged minority party to something between a half-party and a quarter-party. As the Republicans have disappeared, so have most vestiges of two-party government.

The erosion of the GOP in southern New England is so pervasive as to be unprecedented in modern political history. In Connecticut, indicators of trouble are everywhere. After an unsuccessful gubernatorial campaign in 1978, GOP ledgers recorded a deficit of $365,000, the largest in history.[2] A recent fundraiser also illustrates the party's difficulties. In September 1980, Stafford Republicans held a raffle, and the winner was the brother of a former Democratic selectman. His prize: a three-minute romp through a supermarket, where he scooped up over $800 worth of groceries, enough to send the local Republicans scrambling to cover the costs.[3]

For decades the Democrats have been successfully raiding the state's electoral grocery shelves, leaving little for the GOP to choose from. Today Democrats hold all the statewide offices; only once since 1954 have they lost the principal prize, the governorship. Jack Zaiman, former political columnist for the *Hartford Courant*, says it takes an "overwhelming case of [Democratic] incompetence, scandal, wastefulness, deceit, and other wrong-doings" for a Republican to be elected governor.[4] In the congressional races the GOP has fared somewhat better, holding onto one of the U.S. Senate seats and two of Connecticut's six seats in the House.

Disappointing election nights, however, have engendered considerable pessimism among the state's GOP elites: Hartford Republican Chairman Joseph Mozzicato says the party is "scraping the bottom of the barrel";[5] Stafford's GOP chairman facetiously mourns, "God must be a Democrat";[6] House Minority Leader R. E. Van Norstrand says, "We're number three in this state in terms of voter registration, behind the Democrats and the unaffiliated voters. We're like Avis—we just don't have to try harder, we have to try our damnedest."[7]

In Rhode Island, Republican fortunes have so declined that the party's 1980 candidate for governor was heard to remark: "Running in Rhode Island as a Republican is like being the Ayatollah Khomeini at the American Legion Convention."[8] Since 1966 the GOP has been shut out of the governorship. In 1983 four of the five state offices, one of the two congressional seats, and one U.S. Senate seat belong to the Democrats. In the Ocean State, Republicans do not win elections; Democrats lose them.

In Massachusetts things are so dismal for the Republican party that one of its candidates remarked, "Massachusetts is now [just] like Rhode Island."[9] The observation is not far from the mark. Two-party competition is largely nonexistent in the Bay State. Today, for the first time in its history, the party does not occupy any of the six statewide offices, although as recently as 1962 Republicans held three. In Congress the Democrats control both Senate seats and ten of the eleven House seats. The victory of Paul Tsongas in 1978 marked the first time in forty-one years that there was no Massachusetts Republican senator on Capitol Hill.

The deterioration of the Bay State GOP is also reflected in contests for lesser state offices. For thirty-two years the party has not elected a secretary of the commonwealth or state treasurer. Things were so bad in 1974 that the Republican nominee for state treasurer did not obtain the 6,000 signatures required for a place on the November ballot; for the first time the GOP lacked a full slate of statewide candidates. In stark contrast, the Socialist Workers party candidate for that office obtained 50,000 signatures.[10] And this is only one of many Republican "horror stories" in Massachusetts.

Dismal election results have sounded alarums in Massachusetts party circles about the GOP's declining health: Democratic U.S. Representative Barney Frank contends that the Republican party has "sunk from sight";[11] former GOP State Chairman Gordon Nelson says the party is "barely alive";[12] *Boston Globe* columnist Robert Turner writes that the Grand Old Party is "almost functionally extinct";[13] former Governor Frank Sargent is even more colorful, asserting that the Republican party is "lying in ashes";[14] House Democratic Whip John E. Murphy, Jr., neatly sums up the situation: "We have something the Republicans don't have. We have the bodies."[15]

Murphy's observation finds ample illustration in the composition of southern New England's state legislatures. Since the 1970s, when GOP state tickets suffered severe setbacks, the party's legislators have become an endangered species, especially in Massachusetts and Rhode Island. Massachusetts Senate Minority Leader John F. Parker describes the plight: "We are not a minority, we're just the chosen few."[16] This development merits careful attention because the legislature often serves as a training ground for candidates for higher office. In southern New England, the three incumbent governors have served a total of twenty-four years as state legislators. According to Massachusetts Republican State Chairman Andrew Natsios, "The Democrats have always used the legislature as a primary training ground for higher office. We used to do the same thing. But in 1982 we have three Republican legislators running for statewide office. That diminishes our delegation by *10 percent*" (emphasis added).[17]

With every election, Republican legislative performance has provided, in the words of John Chafee, "a bitter barometer" of the political balance.[18] Having lost control of the legislatures in southern New England some years ago, the GOP nevertheless was firmly ensconced as the minority party in these assemblies during the 1960s. Although it lacked a majority during this period, it averaged a respectable share of the legislative vote; in 1966, for example, the GOP received an average 45 percent of the vote in the state Senate contest in Connecticut, 43 percent in Rhode Island, and 34 percent in Massachusetts. Since then, these figures have fallen to precariously low levels. In 1980 the average in Rhode Island was 28 percent and in Massachusetts 12 percent, shocking the Republican hierarchy in both states. After another particularly disappointing election night, a stunned Gordon Nelson surveyed the wreckage: "I had only six seats in the State Senate left and three of these were unopposed, and I thought three were safe. Yet, I even lost one of those. Every election night the Republican party is in worse shape than the one before. We better do something or we'll be gone."[19]

Figures for the state representative contests are not much better. In Massachusetts and Rhode Island the Republicans averaged only 25 percent of the 1980 vote, in sharp contrast to their 1966 showing of 37 and 43 percent, respectively. Democratic majorities have become so massive that the 1978 Massachusetts Republican platform sternly warned about the dangers of "one-party government."[20] GOP losses have been so severe in Massachusetts and Rhode Island that were the party to have a Republican governor elected there would not be enough GOP legislators to sustain a gubernatorial veto.[21]

In Connecticut the Republicans find themselves in considerably better shape, particularly after the 1980 elections. In that year the party's candidates averaged 48 percent of the vote for the state Senate and 47 percent for the House. In 1972 the GOP seized control of both houses of the General Assembly. But despite recent respectable GOP showings, there has been a long-term Democratic trend in the Connecticut legislature. In Fairfield County, for example,

Democrats have so prospered in that longtime Republican strong-
hold that they have their own statehouse caucus. One of the Fairfield Democrats, Ernest Abate, was speaker of the state House of
Representatives.

As the 1970s drew to a close, the Republican party decided in
more and more constituencies not to field candidates for the legislature. In 1980 51 percent of the seats in the Massachusetts House
and 35 percent of those in the Rhode Island House went unchal-
lenged by the GOP; in the state Senates the figures were 75 and 26
percent, respectively.[22] In Connecticut, the number of uncontested
seats has remained small—only 8 percent in its House, none in the
Senate.[23] A better chance of success and the willingness of Republican party members to place their names on the ballot—even as a
last resort—have helped.

There are several reasons for the paucity of GOP candidates in
Massachusetts and Rhode Island, foremost of which is faint hope of
winning or of making even a creditable showing. Former Rhode Island Republican State Chairman Donald Roch says:

A Democratic legislator who has been in office many years is deeply entrenched in his district. He is a popular guy: he leads the parade; he's the
guest speaker at the ham-and-bean breakfast; he puts on a Christmas party
for the poor kids in the district. Relative on top of relative. Patronage on top
of patronage. The only way we're going to win it is if this particular legislator gets into a scandal or he dies. Then we can walk someone in—maybe.[24]

Massachusetts Democratic legislator John E. Murphy, Jr., agrees:

In my district people do not want to run against me for the following reasons: politics is a popularity contest at the legislative level; I am very good
at my job; and I do what I have to do to get elected.
I have had Republican opponents. But no one of substance wants to run
against me because they do not think they can beat me; and they have trouble picking a fight with me on most major issues unless they want to get into
a Reagan–Kennedy type of debate. That kind of ideological discussion,
however, counts for virtually nothing when you are trying to get Joe Jones's
daughter into college or fixing a pothole.[25]

In 1982 Murphy ran unopposed for reelection.

Formidable barriers and quixotic candidacies often result in the selection of GOP candidates who are the Democrats' best possible choices. Surveying their potential Republican opponents, Democratic officials often react with considerable, albeit subdued, glee. Patrick Halley, executive director of the Massachusetts Democratic party, commented in 1979:

The Republican party leaders have sponsored some "turkey" candidates. I probably couldn't have recruited anybody better to run against [incumbent Democratic Attorney General] Frank Bellotti than William Weld. I'd like to tee him off against someone else in the next election. He was a lot of fun. Avi Nelson [conservative GOP candidate for the U.S. Senate] is a lot of fun. He's very visible. You take him out and whack him around a little bit, and Avi reacts just the way you think he is going to react. . . . He's a lot of fun to have around. No threat at the polls.[26]

Given the GOP's current weakness, incumbent Democrats increasingly worry about threats to their security, not from the Republicans but from fellow Democrats. Former U.S. Senator John O. Pastore advises Rhode Island Democrats to "put up a good fight at your primary because that's where the decisions are being made today."[27] Massachusetts Congressman Barney Frank is even more blunt: the only statewide elections that really matter are those for U.S. senator, governor, and attorney general; other decisions have been made in the Democratic primary. Thus, "It is totally irrational, in fact it is stupid, for people to vote in general elections and not in primaries. It would be far more rational instead for people to vote in primaries and not in general elections."[28] As primaries assume increasing importance, voters are faced with a choice not between Democrats and Republicans, but between "in-Democrats" and "out-Democrats."

The GOP did not come upon hard times overnight. A number of complex and interrelated factors, many of which took root during the 1960s, are responsible. During the 1970s these factors coalesced to produce the recent Republican debacles.

One contributing factor in the Republican unraveling has been the party's tendency to nominate its "brighter lights" for higher office. On the face of it, this is a perfectly logical activity for a major party whose goal is to build a majority coalition and win elections;

but in many instances the strategy has backfired. Massachusetts House Minority Leader Frank Hatch lost his bid for the governorship in 1978, and the nominee to succeed him in the legislature lost to a Democratic challenger. Connecticut Republicans have also left many of their most promising candidates stranded after a losing campaign, without a political base to build upon. Former Republican State Chairman Frederick K. Biebel summarizes the party's plight:

In 1974 we sacrificed Bob Steele [the incumbent Republican congressman from the Second Congressional District], who probably could still be in office. . . . He lost [the governorship] and we lost that district. We've done the same thing this time [1978] with Ron Sarasin, who probably could have been reelected without any problem in the Fifth District; and he went forward and gave of himself to run for the governorship for the State of Connecticut.[29]

The dashed aspirations of its politically able are only one element of the GOP malaise. Far more significant is the overall weakness of the state and local organizations. According to Massachusetts GOP State Chairman Natsios:

About one-third of the Republican local organizations in Massachusetts are dead. They never meet; they have nothing in their treasury; they don't support GOP candidates. Another one-third meet occasionally and raise little money, but they are not really active. The remaining one-third are really active—they raise money and support Republican candidates.[30]

Things are not much better in Rhode Island: there a group of Republicans claimed that "various Republican committees are often considered no more than paper tigers and are not viewed as a viable political force."[31]

In many respects the position of the Republican party in southern New England today resembles the one it once occupied in the Old Confederacy. The terms used by V. O. Key to describe southern Republicanism are heard more and more in Connecticut, Massachusetts, and Rhode Island. Calling the GOP an "esoteric cult on the order of a lodge," Key claimed that the main concerns of its leaders lay not in winning elections—that was hopeless—but in gaining and maintaining control of their tiny franchise.[32]

In southern New England this clublike atmosphere has encouraged many Republican town committee members to be more energetic in protecting their own positions than in electioneering. Former Massachusetts Republican State Chairman Nelson describes these political closed shops:

There are a lot of people who would rather be the big fish in a small pond than the little fish in the big pond. . . . We've got people who are in charge of city and town committees who don't do anything, but if you talk about having them step aside for somebody else, they're going to have heart arrest. They would rather have the titles than have it opened up to bring in new people, particularly young people.[33]

The result is an organization largely composed of individuals embedded in their positions and imbued with pessimism about winning elections. As Nelson puts it, "Our problem is that so many people who are active in the city and town committees have been losing for so long that they have a negative outlook."[34]

Given the GOP's "paper tiger" status, its candidates often ignore the party organization and develop their own personal apparatuses. Providence Mayor Vincent Cianci says that an end run around the organization is "a political fact of life":

I can remember going to a Fifth Ward Republican banquet for me a few weeks before the 1974 election. There were more busboys and waiters and waitresses than there were people. . . . If anyone thought that I was going to rely totally upon that organization in the Fifth Ward, then I don't think I would be mayor today. So I had to go beyond the ranks of the Republican organization.[35]

In 1982 Cianci ran for reelection as Mayor as an independent.

Further contributing to the decline of the GOP organizations is the tendency of successful Republican candidates to minimize their party affiliation. When John Volpe ran for governor of Massachusetts, his slogan was "Vote the man, vote Volpe," for which read "Vote the man, not the party." In John Chafee's unsuccessful U.S. Senate bid in 1972, the word *Republican* did not appear in his campaign literature. Lowell Weicker's 1982 reelection slogan was "Nobody's man but yours." In each of these cases the candidate reasoned that the term *Republican* might alienate voters. Rhode Island Republican Don Roch describes his campaign strategy:

I am a salesman. I know how to sell. I know what I can't sell. When I first ran for election in the town of West Warwick, I had to sell Don Roch. That was enough. That was all the people could take. [Yet] . . . I lost. In 1970 I ran for the state Senate. I ran once again selling Don Roch. The third week before the election I added the tag "Republican." Now, if I've sold Don Roch, they can accept the word *Republican*. It's the soft sell.[36]

Instead of promoting their Republicanism, GOP candidates often use the party simply as a vehicle for getting on the ballot. As one elected official in Massachusetts put it over a decade ago, "The Republican Party is a Hertz car we all rent around election time."[37]

Now that the car is almost out of gas, many Republicans are displeased about the inattention and ingratitude of the Republicans in elective office. Typical is the anger expressed by Connecticut State Senate Minority Leader George Gunther toward the GOP's only statewide officeholder: "Lowell Weicker is a loner. He takes the Republican label only at convention time, and then he throws it away. . . . He's a Weicker-liker, and his attitude is, 'To hell with everyone else.' He's the closest thing to a political prostitute as you can be."[38]

How the Republican party is perceived has also become a major liability. The Rhode Island party forthrightly addressed this drawback by establishing the Image Committee in 1977. With unusual candor, the committee admitted that "the image of the Republican Party in Rhode Island is not a good one. . . . Locally as well as nationally, we are perceived as a party of 'againsters,' a party more concerned with the interests of the rich and not the poor, the business executive and not the average consumer, the industrialist and not the environmentalist, those who can help themselves and not those who need help."[39] The "againster" notion is manifest in the other southern New England states as well. Sensing this as a problem in Connecticut, Governor Grasso remarked, "You can't build on negativism. You must have a stronger attraction for an enduring relationship."[40] Former Massachusetts Governor Volpe asserted,

"People will find out soon enough what you are against. But you've got to tell them what you are *for*" (emphasis added).[41]

Another facet of the Republican image is the sense that, in the words of the Image Committee, the GOP is "the voice of Wall Street and the corporate hierarchy in this country. Many voters feel the Party specifically looks after big business interests and legislates in their favor at every opportunity."[42] Rhode Island Democratic State Chairman Rocco Quattrocchi's declaration underscores the GOP problem: "There's a lack of compassion. They're too cold. This is something people sense. They just don't synchronize with the common people."[43] Connecticut's Biebel came out flatly for change: "We've got to care; we've got to be a little more human."[44]

The popular perception of Republicans has proved to be a bonanza for the Democrats. In the words of the Image Committee, "The Democrats take every opportunity to reinforce the image problems that the Republicans have."[45] In a 1979 interview Quattrocchi reasserted a Democratic contention:

I think the Republican party is associated with big business. It's associated with the big oil companies now. It's associated with the big banks and big insurance companies. There is certainly no doubt in my mind that the boards of directors of these companies are Republicans. I think that is common knowledge. . . . [On the other hand] we cater to the little people—the lower- and middle-income people. And they've been satisfied with our performance.[46]

Such claims infuriate many Republicans. A frustrated Chafee complained, "The Democrats can hold a $500-per-plate affair and it's perfectly all right, but if the Republicans hold a $100 affair, it's a rich man's dinner."[47]

Contrary to what seems to be a general belief, the Republican party in southern New England has lost financial support in the business community. Historically, businessmen have been closely identified with the party; a study of the Rhode Island business elite in 1905, for example, revealed that 90 percent of those elected to office were Republicans.[48] Such an alignment helped to foster the still very widespread perception that the Republican party is closely attuned to the interests of its partisans in the private sector. The perception does not square with current reality, according to Warren Johnson, a senior treasury officer at New England Life. Johnson observes that today not one major Boston financial institution is managed by a Brahmin—a group long identified with the GOP:

The Boston Safe and Deposit Company is a good example of the changing social composition of the Massachusetts business community. For many years the firm was managed by John Lowell, a crusty Yankee. He retired eleven years ago. After Lowell left there was a demand for more "professional" managers. Today the firm is a subsidiary of American Express. It is a very different type of company with a very different mindset.[49]

Often businessmen support the Democrats not because of any ideological agreement but out of concern for their economic self-interest. Mayor Cianci's assessment is that

they're opportunists in a lot of instances. They're businessmen first. And they realize that the Democratic party is the strong party. And if they are going to get their grants, and if they are going to get their tax breaks, and if they are going to get their recognition, they have to do business with the Democratic party. And the Democratic party plays hard ball. You're either with them or not with them.[50]

The metamorphosis of the Democratic party into an "Everyone party" does not concern most business leaders, who profess a desire to work with the majority party. Johnson sums up the attitude of most businessmen: "There is little concern among Massachusetts business leaders about reviving the Republican party. Instead, business leaders are more pragmatic. I detect a 'How are we going to make this fly?' orientation. And it does not matter whether it is a King, a Hatch, or a Dukakis who is sitting in the governor's chair."[51] Arthur Lumsden, president of the Greater Hartford Chamber of Commerce, agrees: "The world isn't going to end if either party gets elected. And it isn't going to be saved, either. So it's a matter of working with the 'ins.'"[52]

Corporate support of Democratic candidates also stems from a divergence in views from those of business in other parts of the country. Former Congressman Toby Moffett characterized the southern

New England business community as "enlightened," at variance with its counterparts outside the region.[53] This difference applies particularly to those who represent the new professional class. Johnson's "impression is that a great many of these engineer types are themselves reasonably liberal people. They are not classic business people in that sense. . . . Their politics is out in George McGovern land."[54]

This attitude was reflected in a First National Bank of Boston survey of its newsletter readers in 1979. Businessmen were given a choice between two contrasting ideologies: ideology 1 holds that "the community is no more than the sum of the individuals in it . . . initiative and hard work pay off"; ideology 2 "defines the individual as an inseparable part of a community . . . government plays an important role as the planner and implementer of community needs." When asked which "ideology would be more effective in solving future problems," respondents from the Northeast preferred ideology 1 by a relatively close margin of 53 to 45 percent; respondents elsewhere preferred ideology 1 by more than two to one.[55]

Commenting on these results, Johnson noted that "the free-enterprise, old-line 'less-government-the-better' attitude does not predominate here to the extent it does in traditionally oriented regions."[56]

Although not all segments of the electorate subscribe to every aspect of the negative Republican image, some perceptions have hurt the GOP among southern New England voters. For one thing, its "againster" image has inhibited the GOP's ability to attract majority support in the growing ranks of today's college-educated voters. According to former Massachusetts Governor Sargent, the few college Republicans the party is able to attract are often considered to be "the jokers on campus."[57]

Like so many of the current GOP troubles in southern New England, those with the new class of professionals stem from a prevailing attitude of intellectual distrust in state and national Republican circles. In the 1950s Malcolm Moos observed that "there is more than a grain of truth to the assertion that a large part of the leadership of the Republican party is anti-intellectual to the point of keeping out of its councils valuable human resources. . . . often in key positions to keep a dynamic interest in Republicanism alive in the nation's intellectual centers."[58] Former U.S. Senator Edward Brooke has written that "it is all too apparent that for many Republicans the universities and research centers are a kind of alien, even hostile territory."[59] This attitude exacts a high cost: deprivation of the innovative ideas often generated by the intellectual community. Brooke explains that a "climate of dogmatic incantation" and "oversimplified platitudes" is inhospitable to most intellectual ferment:

By the nature of things, intellectuals are usually in the vanguard of social and economic thought working with new ideas and new solutions. Their seemingly unorthodox proposals often become truisms in a decade. Yet too many Republican leaders have been too quick to dismiss new ideas unworkable, whatever the merits. Too many seem to respect clichés and distrust ideas. . . . Such platitudes have driven the intellectuals from our ranks.[60]

Most professionals follow the intellectuals' lead; thus support for the GOP shrinks still further, and its dwindling membership becomes more doctrinaire and rigid than ever. The closing out of innovative thinking is at the heart of the forces undermining the Republican party in southern New England.

The demise of the Republican party on Beacon Hill is illustrative of the GOP's problem with the new professionals. Once a Yankee bastion, Beacon Hill has in recent years experienced an influx of young middle- and upper-middle-class professional workers. Their presence has dramatically changed the political complexion of this famous Boston ward. In 1932, Beacon Hill voted as a near bloc for Herbert Hoover; forty years later the area gave most of its ballots to George McGovern. Today the Democrats have an advantage there of nearly 4,000 registered voters.

One reason the party has had difficulty on Beacon Hill—and with professionals elsewhere—is its emphasis on orthodox dogmas that most professionals find obsolete. The stronger the Republican party's adherence to ideology, the fewer adherents it has. Political scientist

Walter Dean Burnham has declared that "the smaller a minority becomes, the more likely it is that extreme tendencies will become overrepresented."[61] Governor Dukakis agrees:

As the Democratic party became populated with more and more people who took liberal positions on social and economic issues, where is the constituency for a Sargent and a Hatch? What's left on the Republican side? Well, clearly not too many liberals. Most of these people have either died or joined the Democrats. The younger people who are beginning to swell the ranks of the new voters don't see any reason for sticking to the Republican side of the ledger. As a result, this leaves you with a fairly conservative, traditional Republican constituency.[62]

Thus, the Republicans find themselves in a seemingly unbreakable circle, often firing at themselves instead of at the Democrats. The result is a lost opportunity to make converts among the new professionals. Chester Atkins declares: "Voters are looking for people who are capable of creative thinking and not people who are in an ideological straitjacket."[63] As a result, the Republicans not only reap bitter electoral harvests but also find themselves taken less and less seriously by the professionals.

The Battle for the Franchise: Pragmatic Republicans versus Orthodox Republicans

Compounding the GOP troubles with the professional class is a bitter battle between Orthodox and Pragmatist Republicans for control of the party franchise. Orthodox Republicans subscribe to the view that the party and its candidates should adhere to the principles of a balanced budget, minimal government intervention, and a maximum degree of individual choice. For them these tenets assume the status of religious dogma. And, as in any religion, serious violations of the canons are grounds for excommunication.

Pragmatic Republicans see the party in a completely different light. Foremost among these differences is a willingness to recast the party's traditional dogmas with a view toward winning elections. Obtaining political power, not adhering to party doctrine, is the bottom line of their balance sheet.

Although the Orthodox–Pragmatist struggle hardly reflects the principal fault lines in the electorate as described in chapter 2, it has nevertheless considerably fractured the party's cohesiveness. The intensity of this disruption varies; it is present in both Connecticut and Massachusetts, but is virtually nonexistent in Rhode Island.

In southern New England, Pragmatist Republicans predominate. Many are "old money" Yankees with deep roots in the region; Edgar Litt calls them the "patrician elite."[64] These Republicans, who include the Lodges, Saltonstalls, Hatches, Richardsons, and Chafees, do not generally oppose the goal of winning elections. The view of Rhode Island's Republican State Chairman, John A. Holmes, Jr., is typical: "The bottom line is winning for any political party. What good is orthodoxy if you cannot win? If you win, then your philosophy means something—you can begin to implement your ideas and attract people to your cause. But if you cannot win, what the hell is the point? If the bottom line isn't winning, what is it all about?"[65]

To the Pragmatists, the Orthodox response to these questions is downright foolish. Connecticut House Minority Leader R. E. Van Norstrand sees the ideology as "absolutely, totally unelectable. It will win in a decreasing number of Republican enclaves in this state. But increasingly irrelevant. Wholly irrelevant in the cities. Absolutely unelectable statewide."[66]

The Pragmatists are not simply a group of opportunists with no ideological underpinnings. They want to open up the party to new intellectual currents by emphasizing both the traditional GOP concerns with protection of civil liberties—especially with respect to abortion, homosexuality, and other social and cultural issues—and an economic humanism. Such a strategy is likely to appeal to the region's new professionals. In short, Pragmatists believe the GOP must bend to the demands of the voters.

Lowell Weicker is a leading proponent of a Pragmatist strategy. Keynoting the 1978 Connecticut State Republican Convention, he claimed that the Democratic party's commitment to the disadvantaged had waned in recent years. Invoking Franklin Roosevelt and Hubert Humphrey, Weicker urged the Republicans to act on behalf of the minorities, blue-collar workers, and the cities instead of projecting an image of "a refuge for those who want to hold back history." It would mean de-emphasizing the shibboleths of free enterprise and balanced budgets: "No ledger book is as important as a human being."[67]

Frederick Biebel's outlook is much the same:

You can't go with your head in the sand on every subject and say that government must stay out of everything. I think that might have been true a hundred years ago when we were forming this country. But today if there's a problem such as heating oil . . . and there are families that are going to freeze to death this winter, I'm not against the federal government coming in with a plan to help subsidize those people on an emergency basis.[68]

The Pragmatists' positions on these and other issues have placed them at variance with the national GOP leadership. Last year Weicker was the only Republican U.S. senator to vote against President Reagan's proposed budget cuts.[69]

Other southern New England Republican officeholders have also adopted a decidedly Pragmatist view. An analysis of ratings given to members of the Congress by Americans for Democratic Action (ADA) reveals that, predictably, the region's Democrats receive high marks but also that the region's Republicans rank substantially above Republicans nationwide.[70] As a Massachusetts ADA chairman put it in 1969: "Massachusetts is lucky in having a liberal Republican Party."[71]

National GOP leaders do not feel that Massachusetts—or, for that matter, Connecticut and Rhode Island—are so lucky. In 1964 presidential candidate Barry Goldwater suggested that the eastern seaboard be allowed to "float out to sea"; no doubt he was thinking at least in part of southern New England.[72] Since then, southern New England has generally been on the losing side in GOP presidential nominations.[73] Commenting on the divergence, Rhode Island Chairman Holmes notes that his state's Republican philosophy differs considerably from the views expressed by President Reagan.[74] Most of the region's Republican congressional representatives—Claudine Schneider, Lawrence DeNardis, Silvio Conte, Margaret Heckler,

Stewart McKinney—joined ranks with the so-called Gypsy Moths in the Ninety-Seventh Congress.

Orthodox Republicans subscribe to a far different party ideal; rather than winning elections, adherence to the traditional dogmas of free enterprise, minimal government intervention in the economy and in the life of the individual, and a commitment to a balanced budget is the overriding concern. The 1974 Massachusetts platform asserted:

We reject the emerging philosophy that the political process is merely a strategy game in which the attainment and maintenance of power are the only objectives. We likewise reject the concomitant notion that a political party's sole function is to provide the resources and manpower needed to win elections.

Rather we believe that the political process should be . . . a vehicle through which a large number of like-minded citizens can formulate a set of sound principles of government, attract candidates who share these principles, suggest which programs emanating from these principles best serve the needs of society, present the principles, candidates and programs to the public for approval, and continue to provide policy guidance between elections.[75]

The rigid Orthodox stance has provoked a "love it or leave it" attitude among party members: Orthodoxy requires that candidates either conform to the canons of the faith or risk excommunication. Of concomitant importance is the use of the party platform to expound the Orthodox approach to present-day problems. To this group, the Connecticut example of not issuing a party platform in 1978 comes very near heresy. State Central Committeeman Fenton Futtner explained that decision: "It was felt that the position of the Party doesn't necessarily correspond to the thoughts of a particular candidate running as Republican."[76] Such reasoning is anathema to the Orthodox faction.

Orthodox Republicanism traces its roots to the presidential candidacy of U.S. Senator Robert Taft in 1952, but it was not until 1964 that the faction seized control of the national convention and nominated a candidate who subscribed to the Orthodox viewpoint. Political scientists Nelson Polsby and Aaron Wildavsky were among the first to recognize that Goldwater attracted many Republicans who shared his commitment to Orthodox principles; they ascribed three characteristics to the "purists": conformity to a set of principles, rejection of most forms of political compromise, and lack of orientation to winning the election. As one Goldwater delegate said, "I would rather be one against 20,000 and believe I was right."[77] Since 1964, Orthodox Republicanism has grown both nationally and in southern New England. Referring to the faction in a national sense, Weicker has observed that "my party would do far better in the election of a pope than a president of the United States."[78]

Orthodox Republicans account for only a tiny minority in the region, yet their influence in party affairs is far greater than their numbers suggest. Orthodox strength, according to Connecticut House Minority Leader Van Norstrand, resides in those who give money to the campaigns: "The financial contributors are making an investment, and some want a return on their dollar. They want to call the shots. Sometimes Republican candidates have to make difficult choices; and if the checkwriters do not agree with a philosophy, financial support will be withheld."[79]

The Orthodox Republican presence in Connecticut has left the Pragmatic wing of the party discouraged and frustrated. According to Van Norstrand, "The idea that we have to have some loyalty oath checklist, and if you don't check off every item you are off the loyalty list is impossible, because that's not where the electorate is."[80] He pessimistically asks,

How many times do we have to go through a somber election eve? Do we finally make up our minds that we are going to listen to the electorate and go through a happy election eve? We must try to win, and stop being hung up because the best person to win that time might be a liberal school board member—liberal, so-called, because he supports spending for education. That person may have a built-in constituency that can win elections.

Nevertheless, I envision more somber election eves. I don't know why— it seems obvious to me. But what is obvious to me is heresy to others. And I don't understand that. I never will.[81]

In Rhode Island the Pragmatist view is without serious challenge. Most intraparty disputes center on personalities, not on ideology.

As former Rhode Island House Minority Leader Frederick Lippitt declares, to participate in a losing campaign on behalf of an Orthodox candidate is a "very expensive, time-consuming process to engage in for principles that are meaningless."[82] Thus, in Rhode Island the overriding goal continues to be the seizure of political power through winning elections, at which the Republicans have been notably inept in recent years. Recovery, even in the absence of ideological struggle, will be difficult, as Holmes acknowledges: "It is going to be a slow process. People in this state still see the GOP as a negative group of people. . . . And we need a great deal of adrenalin to get the ball rolling."[83]

If the Orthodox presence is minimal in Connecticut and nonexistent in Rhode Island, it is very much alive in Massachusetts. A weakened GOP has made the party ripe for an Orthodox assault. By the end of the 1970s a series of events had catapulted Orthodox Republicans into the leadership of the Massachusetts Republican party. The signs of that takeover are everywhere: the predominance of Orthodox Republicans on the State Central Committee, the election of one of their number in 1976 to the state chairmanship, the Orthodox challenge to incumbent GOP Governor Sargent in 1974, and the nomination in 1978 of an Orthodox gubernatorial candidate. In the forefront of the Orthodox challenge has been former GOP State Chairman Gordon Nelson.

Gordon Nelson's political background is that of a classic Orthodox Republican. A member of Young Americans for Freedom, he campaigned vigorously for Goldwater in 1964. In 1971 he and other former members of Young Americans for Freedom assembled the New Right Coalition, an organization of political "radicals" whose philosophical cornerstone was a firm belief in absolute laissez-faire capitalism.[84] Nelson was again visibly active in 1974, concentrating his energies on the gubernatorial campaign of Carroll Sheehan, like Nelson a Republican of the Orthodox stripe, in the formidable task of challenging the incumbent governor, Republican Frank Sargent. Sargent, a Pragmatist, had drawn the wrath of many Orthodox Republicans while in office. Although Sargent had decisively defeated

Sheehan in the GOP contest, he had allocated half his campaign chest to the primary. This internal warfare helped Democrat Dukakis defeat Sargent in November.

More important, Sargent's loss set in motion a chain of events that culminated in the election of Nelson to the GOP state chairmanship. Traditionally, one of the prerogatives of an incumbent governor is to select the chairman, a choice routinely ratified by the state committee. Sargent's chairman was a man with whom he was politically comfortable, but defeat at the polls considerably reduced his influence in party affairs. Recognizing this diminution of power, Nelson decided to go after the top party rung. Calling himself a "leader of an insurrection," Nelson fought a bitter battle with the Pragmatists, emerging victorious by a scant two votes.[85] Nelson explains:

The Sargent faction of the Republican party tried to have no distinction between the two political parties. Sargent was a "me-too" Republican. . . . I believe that the Republican party must stand for something. . . . If we are 14.5 percent of the electorate in this state, we must give the other 85.5 percent a reason why they should be Republicans. We should give them issues whereby they can distinguish us from the opposition.[86]

As chairman, Nelson adhered to the narrow path of political behavior prescribed by Orthodox Republicanism. In 1978 the Massachusetts platform energetically defended the principle of laissez faire. At the state convention Nelson successfully engineered the nomination to the governorship of a little-known Orthodox Republican, Edward F. King. Although Pragmatist Hatch defeated King in the primary, Hatch blames the Orthodox Republicans for his own defeat in the general election: "As it was, we received 47 percent of the vote by attracting more than three Democrats or independents for every Republican. If the party faithful had been rallied to our cause, I would have had more than the 50,000 votes to win."[87] Nelson did try to emphasize to his conservative following the need to win elections, but they resisted the seemingly obvious. According to Nelson, "The bottom line is winning. That's what conservatives haven't understood. . . . It does no good to tilt at windmills. It is time we grew up."[88] Nelson's words present the ultimate irony of a state party chairman trying to persuade his followers of the importance of winning elections.

Nelson, however, has shown no sign of deviating from his Orthodox principles. In late 1979 he began trying to secure slots for Orthodox candidates on the 1980 state committee. (Under Massachusetts law, selection of state committee members is held in conjunction with the GOP presidential primary.) In this endeavor Nelson encountered bitter opposition from the Pragmatists, who had long dominated the state organization. In a state committee meeting after the presidential primary, Nelson was ousted by a scant two-vote margin. Much of Nelson's defeat can be blamed on the large numbers of Democrats who crossed party lines and voted for John Anderson, then a Republican candidate in the presidential primary. Anderson backers, along with some George Bush supporters, supported Pragmatic candidates for state committee slots.

The divisions remain fairly deep. Most Pragmatist Republicans strongly oppose the strategy of the Nelson cohort. Hatch, for example, believes that backing Orthodox Republicans in heavily Democratic Massachusetts has had "tragic consequences" for the party and cites his campaign as one casualty:

My campaign attracted a unique political coalition, one which is now destined for inevitable collapse. . . . They weren't just the liberals to whom Nelson objected so violently. They were Democrats and independents of all persuasions, backgrounds, and age groups. . . .
If he [Nelson] had moved aggressively to keep E. F. King and his cohorts in line, there is a good chance that many of these groups would be participating in the renaissance of the Republican party today. But, instead, the party is more ragged and impotent than ever.[89]

In 1980 Hatch refused to go along with longtime Reagan supporter Nelson and instead endorsed John Anderson for president in the general election.

Sargent is even more critical of Nelson and his Orthodox followers, calling them "a bunch of turkeys and cuckoos."[90] To Sargent the Orthodox ideology represents an unrealistic attempt to turn back the pages of history: "Those damn slogans! They're all great but try to implement them; they're ridiculous."[91] What angers Sargent most is the unwillingness of the Orthodox to tolerate any attempt at forging a political accommodation: "The word *compromise* in Gordon Nelson's little world isn't a word. You are not supposed to do that. It's sacrilegious or something. . . . You can't win elections or run the government if you don't understand the word *compromise*. It shouldn't be a dirty word."[92]

Harsh words like Sargent's are not uncommon among Massachusetts Democrats. But divisiveness within the state's "Everyone party" is not life-threatening. Republican State Representative Iris K. Holland is succinct: "The Democrats practice cannibalism, just as we do"; the only difference is that once they satisfy their appetites "there are always some Democrats left over."[93] As the Republican maneaters continue to tear at each other, the probability increases that the party will be completely devoured.

Some suggest that the GOP may already have fallen victim. A former Hatch volunteer, Ronald Civins-Mills, says flatly:

The Republican party in Massachusetts does not exist. . . . It is pretty much in the position of the Republican party in Mississippi in 1956. It's nonexistent. And it will just simply fall off the end of the earth. And it will be that way for a long time because there aren't any power centers interested in reviving it or [that] have the capability of reviving it. Some of those people who are interested are ideologues and they don't have enough strength. And they haven't figured out who it is they're supposed to be talking to. They're more worried about talking to each other than about talking to the people. And I don't see any change in that situation for a long time. So, I expect to see a flat line for the Republican party in Massachusetts: it's dead.[94]

House Speaker "Tip" O'Neill agrees with Civins-Mills: "I do not see any future for the Republican party in Massachusetts. There is no one on the horizon who can dig them out of their current difficulties."[95]

There have been several suggestions as to how to shore up the sagging Republican fortunes. Sargent, for example, would rename the party the "Independent Republicans."[96] Yet a cosmetic change such as this would do little to solve the GOP dilemma. By 1980 Republicans in Massachusetts and Rhode Island had declined to a minority status roughly equivalent to that of the Democrats at the turn of the century.[97] In Connecticut, a better chance of winning and minimal Orthodox–Pragmatist struggles have improved the GOP's standing, but there, too, the party remains weak.

The minority status of the Republicans today, however, is fundamentally different from that of the Democrats eight decades ago. Although the national Democratic party was split between agrarian and immigrant branches, Democrats in southern New England almost without exception aligned themselves squarely with the latter. The immigrants proved to be a sturdy branch, providing the Democrats with a sound geographic base upon which to build the party fortunes. In 1900, for example, virtually all the Democratic state legislators represented urban districts. As the immigrant numbers increased, so did Democratic strength, with the party attaining majority status by the 1930s.

Today's Republican party is in a far worse position. One obstacle is the bitter ideological dispute between the Pragmatist and Orthodox camps. Today the Orthodox challenge poses a "clear and present danger" to the GOP; it not only precludes the unified stance so necessary to a minority, but also projects a disproportionate strength. The Orthodox faction is a very weak reed for the party to lean on because it is considerably at variance with the fastest-growing segment of the electorate, the professionals. As the ranks of this new class gain electorally, the Republican party is increasingly associated with a die-hard mentality that finds its most frequent expression in Orthodox views.

This is not to say that the GOP is likely to expire any time soon. Electoral laws assuring the party of access to the ballot have seen to that. But the prospect is one of a sustained struggle between the Pragmatist and Orthodox wings of the party. Given their increasingly straitened circumstances, the question for the Republicans is which of these factions will control the franchise.

5

THE STAGING OF POLITICAL CONFLICT

The prevailing social and cultural tide in southern New England raises two very important considerations: the form the continuing professional and blue-collar conflict will take, and the ability of the region's political and governmental institutions to deal with that conflict.

Harvard University's John Kain argues that New England has no resources other than its people and imagination. According to Kain, if the Pilgrims had somehow found their way to Santa Barbara instead of Plymouth Rock, New England would be an economic wasteland.[1] But this did not happen, and the future of the region's economy is in the direction of increased professionalism. The scars from the exodus of the immigrant industries during the first half of the century have largely healed. In Massachusetts and Connecticut the new professional-based industries seem firmly in place. Ray Stata, president of the Massachusetts High Technology Council, believes the state's high-tech industries will continue to expand because "the degree of advancement for high-technology will be in direct proportion to the quality of the universities supporting it."[2] Agreeing with Stata is former Connecticut Governor John N. Dempsey, who holds that a state's educational facilities are the key to its economic future.[3]

Only in Rhode Island is professionalization lagging. Textron's Erskine White explains: "For a variety of reasons . . . stemming from its early days in textiles and its relatively small-scale . . .

jewelry-based industry, we have had a fairly low-technology and therefore low-wage but important industry in Rhode Island."[4] Warren Johnson, senior treasury officer at New England Life, agrees with White: "Home-grown businesses are what is unique about the New England region. What Rhode Island needs to attract are the new businesses starting out—for example, a university professor with a new idea. But Rhode Island has not created the right type of embryonic environment for these businesses."[5]

Quality institutions of higher learning are only one factor attracting professionally based industries to southern New England. The abundance of vacant land and of old mills waiting to be developed, available capital, and a quality of life that many people find attractive are singular and appealing assets in all three states. To use them beneficially is of primary importance, argues the *New England Economic Review*: "The prospects for the future depend on whether New England's unique advantage will be competed away by newer centers such as Palo Alto than on state government incentive programs and tax breaks. Just how to hold on to that advantage is what we should be pondering."[6]

Retaining its advantage is indeed one of the major tasks facing southern New England in the next decade. The new professional class is emerging in several areas—particularly the upper Midwest, the Pacific Northwest, and the so-called Silicon Valley near Palo Alto. The professional cadre has taken hold in Minnesota as well as in Massachusetts and Connecticut. *Time* reports that in the past decade it "has become one of the nation's leading 'brain industry' centers—more than 170 electronic and related technical businesses now employ more than 70,000 people. . . ."[7] The forces encouraging increased professionalization elsewhere are the same as those at work in southern New England: respected universities, available capital, unused land, and a quality of life that appeals to many. In 1980 the dean of the University of Minnesota's Institute of Technology advocated establishment of Minnesota, Inc., a formal linkage between the state's university and high-technology industry. To help in the formation of the program, Control Data Corporation, a major computer employer, has invested $2 million to develop a computer sciences center at the university.[8]

Such formal arrangements between universities and industries dependent upon professionals are one sign of the increased role that higher education will play in the continued professionalization of the electorate. Another is a recent ABC News/Louis Harris survey that highlighted the desirability of a college degree today: 72 percent of the respondents believed that level of education will become more essential to careers during the 1980s.[9]

Politically, the Democratic party has been the beneficiary of the increased professionalization of the electorate. Among most demographic groups and in every section of the country, Democrats maintain supremacy over Republicans (see table 5 in the appendix). Although the Republicans have a marginal lead among college-educated professionals, their commitment to the GOP is lukewarm, as is demonstrated in their willingness in recent years to vote for Democratic candidates. In 1978 Democratic congressional candidates received 53 percent of the professional vote; in 1936, 42 percent.[10]

As elsewhere in the nation, the Democrats' appeal to the professionals has increased the party's electoral strength in southern New England. According to Connecticut Governor William O'Neill, "The Democratic party is at its strongest point in history."[11] Jack Zaiman, former political columnist for the *Hartford Courant*, observes, "There is no sign of the Democratic trend breaking up."[12] Only when the party is unable to manage the professional and blue-collar fracture is a climate created for divisive intra-party confrontations, as in the 1978 King–Dukakis contest. According to Michael Dukakis, "For a good long while [we] will be dominated by *a* party. That party will tend to have a lot of bits and pieces within it and will become an umbrella more than a narrowly defined ideological party. And the question the Democrats will have to answer is, can we stand the prosperity?"[13]

If the Democrats have prospered from the rise of the professionals, they have been fortuitous beneficiaries. The distancing of the

Republicans from the new class has left the latter with few alternatives. In commenting on the French political scene, Maurice Duverger has observed that "the decline of official religions coincides with the rise of political religions."[14] A somewhat kindred phenomenon is affecting the Republican party. Aside from electoral decline, the most significant development for the GOP in the past two decades has been the changing nature of the party itself. Clinton Rossiter has described the American parties as traditionally "creatures of compromise . . . vast, gaudy, friendly umbrellas under which all Americans whoever and wherever and however minded they may be are invited to stand for the sake of being counted in the next election."[15] Orthodox Republicans, however, violate Rossiter's claim. Rather than adhering to the concept of a cadre party—that is, a group of activists operating under a broad ideological mandate and engaged in attracting public support for their party's candidates— Orthodox Republicans are behaving like a mass membership party, which emphasizes ideological agreement with a definitive list of principles.

The resultant bickering between the Orthodox and Pragmatist wings has not helped any of the Republican state parties with the electorate, especially with its fastest-growing segment, the professionals. The new professional class regards such controversies over strategy and principles as outdated and of no consequence. Connecticut House Minority Leader R. E. Van Norstrand comments:

I find many times that the establishment of the party has narrower horizons on how to address the public agenda. My problem is that I find the breadth of these horizons largely unelectable. You reach a point where you say either you are going to be a majority and win, or you are going to be an increasingly irrelevant minority, perhaps ideologically more defined, but irrelevant.[16]

Emerging from the GOP difficulties is a weak one-and-a-half party system. The Democrats, though numerically dominant, lack the organizational resources necessary to discipline the flow of the new social and cultural tide.

In the view of E. E. Schattschneider, "The crucial problem in politics is the management of the conflict."[17] In southern New England the outlook for management by the parties varies. Massachusetts Democratic State Chairman Chester Atkins has characterized the prospects of that state's party apparatus to deal with future professional and blue-collar battles as "bleak."[18] In Connecticut the parties are in a better position, although there, too, U.S. Senator Christopher Dodd sees a danger of fracturing:

There is no question that there is a real potential for erosion as the traditional base of the Democratic party, the working people, hear issues that were not discussed before. You did not discuss abortion twenty years ago. Even the death penalty was a relatively esoteric topic. . . . And there will be some erosion [in Democratic support among blue-collar workers]—and you are going to see some of it in the next few years.[19]

Unlike their neighbors, Rhode Islanders enjoy continued consensus on most social and cultural issues. There the agreement results from the dominance of blue-collar workers, not from strong party organizations.

Party organizations, both in southern New England and nationally, are incredibly weak. Even states with a reputation for strong parties, like Connecticut, have not been immune. Democratic State Chairman James Fitzgerald describes what is left of the once-mighty party organization that John Bailey built: "We do not have a sophisticated staff in terms of numbers or expertise in the sense that we do not have someone from MIT. We have two ladies, a part-time executive director, and a man who runs our equipment. That's our staff."[20]

Andrew Natsios, the Massachusetts Republican chairman, points out that the political parties "no longer act as an intermediary between elected officials and the voters. That function has been taken over by the news media."[21] Massachusetts Lieutenant Governor Thomas P. O'Neill III agrees: "The media today are the equivalent of the old-fashioned ward bosses. And they are the principal reason for the demise of two-party politics. And we are still institutionally grappling with this development in order to understand our new professional role."[22] Indeed, political parties are losing most of their functions. Natsios comments:

It used to be that the political parties were intermediaries between the voters and the politicians; they used to nominate people for office at conventions; they used to dole out patronage; they used to raise money for candidates.

They don't do those things any more. Patronage has declined; the media [have] become the link between the voter and the politician; and the convention has given way to the direct primary. The functions of the old party structures are gone.[23]

The decline of the political parties creates a new problem for the American political system—namely, the staging of political conflict. During the ethnocultural and New Deal tides, the parties generally possessed the necessary resources to manage the tidal flow. Party leaders acted as conduits for the contending collectivities. In short, the parties provided a stage upon which the opposing Catholic and Protestant interests could act out their disagreements. Clinton Rossiter has noted: "It has been [the parties'] historic mission to hold the line against some of the most powerful centrifugal forces in American society. . . . If the parties continue to do their political, social, and historic tasks with modest effectiveness, we need have few qualms about moving into the future with our pluralized form of government."[24]

Today the parties are managing conflict with less than "modest effectiveness." Filling the vacuum in an America "beyond parties" are two phenomena: professional campaign consultants and the electronic media.

Professional campaign managers are not new. During the past two decades, however, media consultants, polltakers, and the businessman-as-campaign-tactician have replaced the party "pols." These campaign-science experts were well represented in Ronald Reagan's 1980 presidential bid: Stuart Spencer, Reagan's manager, is president of a political consulting firm in California; Richard Wirthlin, Reagan's polltaker, manages Decision Making Information, a survey research firm; Peter Dailey, Reagan's media adviser, is in charge of Dailey and Associates, an advertising agency. Jimmy Carter and John Anderson also had phalanxes of campaign experts. Together, the professional political consultants and the electronic media have created a "double-bind" that is undermining the American political system. Now the professional tacticians often exploit rather than manage conflict, particularly when it involves the new social and cultural agenda. Edward J. King deliberately exacerbated existing tensions in the Massachusetts electorate. One of King's campaign workers succinctly summarized his 1978 strategy: "We put all the hate groups into one big pot and let it boil."[25] As governor, King found himself unable to establish linkages to voters outside his winning coalition. James Howell believes King never really tried to bridge the gap.[26] Edward Reilly, a policy analyst for King, described the new realities:

The fractures present in the Massachusetts electorate make it very difficult to govern. There were single issue groups who went to the polls in 1978 and voted on the abortion issue, on the death penalty, et cetera. And those voters will always be there.

I think it is very unfortunate right now in American politics that people have become intolerant. They must learn to recognize that an elected official must serve diverse groups. There is a banana republic mentality among the voters nationally.[27]

Professional tacticians, polltakers, and the media have exploited the "banana republic mentality" in the electorate by arousing social and cultural tensions. One victim of this strategy, Dukakis, comments:

The use of polltakers in an effort to segment the electorate is a skillful effort to patch together a negative coalition. That is what Dressler, Morris, and Tortorello [King's pollsters] did for King in 1978. On primary day people said, "I am going to vote for King because of his position on abortion, the death penalty, et cetera." . . . So negative campaigning is a strategy that is out there and is being used all the time. And it can hurt you if you do not respond.[28]

The favored instrument of campaign scientists for exploiting tensions is the electronic media. As Dukakis notes, "Today the electronic media have made it possible for candidates to pursue a negative strategy with far greater impact. Twenty years ago handcards or fliers would not have had the same effect."[29] Reilly agrees:

The electronic media can effectively bypass the parties today. They can go right into your home and say, "That fellow who you think is a clean-cut congressman voted to kill these dead babies over here in the trashcan." They can grab you while you're sitting there with your wife and your seven-year-old watching Walt Disney with that message. This is something that they could not do before. A candidate or party would have had to get volunteers to mail this literature, or would have to go on a door-to-door campaign.[30]

As the campaign scientists and media experts continue to exploit what remains of the parties, the survival of the political system is jeopardized. The political system is not self-supporting. Rather, it is sustained by four distinct pillars that share responsibility: the parties, the executive branch, the legislative branch, and the judiciary. Today the party column is substantially weakened; in Massachusetts it may already have collapsed. Whether the remaining three entities will share an increased responsibility for management of the new social and cultural issues depends upon the composition of the workforce and the strength of the party system. If the workforce is highly professionalized and the party system is weak, as in Massachusetts, social and cultural conflict will proliferate.

COMPOSITION OF WORKFORCE	STRONG PARTY SYSTEM	WEAK PARTY SYSTEM
High percentage of professional and technical workers	Social and cultural conflict minimized (Connecticut)	Social and cultural conflict maximized (Massachusetts)
Low percentage of professional and technical workers	Social and cultural conflict minimized	Social and cultural conflict minimized; factions emerge (Rhode Island)

Intensification of social and cultural disputes places an enormous strain on the other pillars supporting the political system. The executive branch, for instance, has suffered from the parties' weakness as amateurs gain preeminence within them. King's attainment of the Massachusetts governorship is a direct consequence of the collapse of the party organizations in that state.

Legislative support for the political system also becomes strained. As the parties have become weaker, legislators have had to cope with the new social and cultural issues without benefit of prior party management. This is a far cry from existing conditions during the ethnocultural and New Deal tides, when legislators ratified their party platforms or submitted to strong, party-oriented executive leadership. Even party leaders in the legislatures—like their counterparts in the party organizations—are often unable to guide the debate. Filling the vacuum has been a proliferating number of committees and subcommittees. The staging of the new social and cultural conflicts before these multitudinous bodies often exacerbates tensions between professional and blue-collar workers.

Realizing the potential for divisiveness, most legislators prefer to avoid confronting the social and cultural issues. John E. Murphy, Jr., a Democratic whip in the Massachusetts House of Representatives, comments: "These are emotional issues. There is really no way I can work the floor of the Massachusetts House to affect the death penalty or abortion. Legislators try to keep these issues locked up if they can. A good leader would not get involved in these social and cultural issues."[31]

As a result of legislative avoidance, dissatisfied interests on both sides turn to the judiciary to settle the issues. Judges are asked to assume a management role they once shared with party leaders. Far from resolving the controversies, however, court decisions usually have opened a political Pandora's box. Almost ten years after the Supreme Court's ruling in *Roe* v. *Wade* making abortion in the first trimester legal, circumventing congressional legislation, a proposed "Right-to-Life" amendment, and public demonstrations on both sides continue.

The use of the judiciary as a "stage" for airing blue-collar and professional disagreements has institutionally strained the courts and damaged their prestige. From 1966 to 1979, public confidence in the U.S. Supreme Court declined sharply, from 50 percent to 28 percent.[32] Among the non-college-educated, 30 percent expressed a great deal of confidence in 1973, compared with 26 percent in 1978.

During the same period, however, those with a college education or more gained confidence: 39 percent in 1973, 43 percent in 1978.[33] The 17 percent differential probably results from the Court's tendency to support the professionals' social and cultural views.

These strains on political and governmental institutions have made the electorate less ready than formerly to grant legitimacy to each of the pillars. A recent Massachusetts survey revealed that 40 percent of the state's voters believe that "instead of being the servants of the people, elected officials in Massachusetts really are *the enemy of the people*" (emphasis added).[34] Nationally, support levels for most government and other institutions, which dropped significantly from 1966 to 1971 (no doubt in connection with the Vietnam conflict), have declined steadily ever since.[35] Similarly, the proportion of those expressing a "great deal of confidence" in state government dropped from 24 percent in 1973 to 15 percent in 1978.[36]

The weakening of the party column—in what up to now has been a sturdy support system—places an increased burden on the remaining pillars: the executive, the legislatures and the judiciary. Clearly, these tensions must be eased.

Restoration of the political parties as a "stage" where political conflicts can be aired appears to be unlikely. James Howell believes that although the economic transition is virtually complete, the parties are unable or unwilling to take the political risks necessary to manage the new tide:

I am more pessimistic about these social and cultural divisions than ever before. We have an opportunity to play a major role and ameliorate the differences that exist, yet I think those differences are as significant as they have ever been. In fact, I think the divisions are going to get worse.

We have got to provide some leadership here. We cannot put everyone's hate into a bag and start shaking it up. We need someone to afflict the comfortable. And that type of leadership can come from the governor. If you do not have an effective redistribution of income, then you are going to play into existing tensions in the areas of abortion, crime, et cetera. . . . This process does not involve taking economic chances. But it does involve taking some political risks. And having the guts to take political risks is much harder than taking the economic risks.[37]

To break the vicious cycle of institutional weaknesses requires a refurbishing of the political parties. Connecticut's "challenge primary" law provides one model for party restoration. Another means of enhancing the party system would be to give them complete control over all campaign finances, with limits attached according to the office at stake. U.S. House Speaker Thomas P. O'Neill believes that just such a measure would be "the greatest thing that could happen to strengthen the party. . . ."[38] Pollsters, media consultants, and other campaign professionals ought to be encouraged to devote their talents to the political parties, rather than individual candidates. Unless these measures are undertaken, we face the prospect of more candidacies like King's on both sides of the social and cultural issues. And the prospect of a social and cultural tide running out of control is chilling.

Postscript

THE 1982 ELECTIONS

Personalities changed: "in Democrat" Edward J. King was replaced by "out Democrat" Michael S. Dukakis; eight-term Massachusetts Republican Congresswoman Margaret Heckler was ousted by Democrat Barney Frank; and Connecticut newcomer Bruce Morrison snatched the congressional seat held by Republican Lawrence De Nardis.

But many familiar faces remained: Massachusetts Democrat Edward M. Kennedy was returned to the U.S. Senate for the fifth time; two Republican U.S. Senators—John Chafee and Lowell Weicker— clung to their seats by insubstantial pluralities; and Democratic governors J. Joseph Garrahy and William A. O'Neill won by comfortable margins as did most of their ticket mates. Most state legislators in the region were reelected, and they were joined by some new Democratic faces. Whereas Massachusetts and Rhode Island continued to retain their one-party Democratic reputations, a greater degree of party competition was evident in Connecticut.

The presence of Ronald Reagan, who did not face reelection in 1982, was felt everywhere. While Reagan urged voters to "stay the course," politicians traded barbs about the wisdom of "Reaganomics," with most southern New England Republicans preferring to distance themselves from the president. When Barney Frank accused Margaret Heckler of supporting "everything Mr. Reagan wanted until early this year," she retorted: "I am not a clone [of Ronald Reagan]."[1] Rhode Island Democratic U.S. Senate nominee,

Julius Michaelson, also tried to portray his opponent as a Reaganite: "Republican Ronald Reagan can count on Republican John Chafee."[2] GOP congressional candidate Nancy Johnson, a former co-chair of Reagan's 1980 presidential campaign in Connecticut, also complained that her Democratic opponent "tries to paint me as a Reagan clone."[3] Even Democrats could not resist "cloning" other members of their party with the Reagan appellation: Michael Dukakis consistently reminded Massachusetts voters that Ed King was "Ronald Reagan's favorite Democratic governor."[4]

If one views the election results as a referendum on Reaganomics, the southern New England returns provide little encouragement to Reagan. Most Republicans lost; and the few who won—notably Weicker and Chafee—prided themselves on their independence of the president and his party. Surveying the results, Democratic pollster Peter Hart commented: "Ronald Reagan and New England mix as well as oil and water."[5]

To view the election as a referendum on Reaganomics, however, is just plain wrong. At stake in this election was more than whether or not the electorate approved of Reagan's domestic policies. Rather, the enduring currents in the tide of politics dominate the election story. As Samuel Lubell remarked several years ago, "More than any other single factor voting is dominated by continuity with the past, being truly like a river that rises in the past and empties into the future."[6] Continuity with the past—not a rejection of the present—is the message of the 1982 vote in southern New England.

Massachusetts: Divided Democrats, Enfeebled Republicans

A few weeks after election day, Senator Edward M. Kennedy observed: "The Democratic party's future in Massachusetts is bright. . . . We have an extraordinary array of talent."[7] Kennedy is right. In 1982, Massachusetts Democrats captured every statewide office, ten of eleven congressional seats, and even improved upon their mammoth margins in the state legislature. These Democratic victories, however, came at the end of a long year of bitter intraparty squabbling—much of it centering around the Democratic primary for governor.

The "Rematch": King versus Dukakis

In January 1979 when Michael Dukakis walked down the statehouse steps for the last time as governor, most political observers believed there would be a "rematch" between Dukakis and the man who beat him in the 1978 Democratic gubernatorial primary, Edward J. King. Many Dukakis Democrats, particularly the professionals, savored the possibility of beating their nemesis. That possibility was enhanced by the charges of corruption that swirled around the King administration—accusations that intensified when King's transportation secretary received a seven-to-ten year jail term for bribery.[8] Massachusetts Democrats were ready to declare the rematch a "no contest." Dukakis led King in the early rounds by an incredible 56 percent.[9] So disliked was King that voters ranked him 149th among the 150 U.S. senators and governors—just below California's S. I. Hayakawa, but slightly above New Jersey's embattled Harrison Williams.[10] Peter Y. Flynn, King's campaign manager, described the enormous political difficulties the governor faced at the beginning of the campaign:

Our early polls showed that the people felt Dukakis had done a better job than Governor King on every single issue: crime, taxes, welfare, jobs. A clincher was the question of who had done a better job on fuel assistance, Michael Dukakis or Edward King. The respondents answered Dukakis. *But Michael Dukakis never had a fuel assistance program*. (Emphasis added.)[11]

King refused to concede. But at the end of the campaign, Dukakis beat him 54 to 46 percent.

Clearly, other factors helped King remain in contention—chief among these his emphasis on social and cultural issues. This agenda, continued to polarize Massachusetts Democrats in 1982. A survey conducted at the Democratic State Convention reveals the profound disagreements between Dukakis and King supporters on these issues: 28 percent of Dukakis's delegates opposed using state funds for abortion compared with 84 percent of King's backers. Thirty-eight percent of Dukakis supporters favored reinstating the death penalty for persons convicted of first degree murder, while 74 percent of King delegates supported such a proposal. An overwhelming 89 percent of Dukakis supporters favored passage of the Equal Rights Amendment, while only half of the King delegates agreed. Seventy-six percent of King's backers said there were no circumstances under which they would vote for a gubernatorial candidate "who *opposed* minimum jail sentences for violent crimes"; 52 percent said they could not support a candidate "who *opposed* the death penalty"; 63 percent said they could not endorse a nominee "who *favored* abortion."[12] In each instance, these were Michael Dukakis's positions.

Other life-style issues also intruded. On the question of premarital sex 31 percent of King delegates believed it to be "always wrong" compared with 11 percent of Dukakis supporters. Extramarital sex and homosexuality also divided the two groups. Seventy-two percent of King's delegates thought extramarital sex was "always wrong"; 36 percent of Dukakis's backers agreed. Similarly, 74 percent of King's supporters condemned homosexuality as opposed to 37 percent of Dukakis's delegates.[13]

While Dukakis concentrated on King's ties to Reagan and emphasized his own corruption-free performance in office, King followed his successful 1978 strategy of stressing his social and cultural views. And the plan nearly worked. In those areas where blue-collar workers still predominate King out-performed Dukakis: in South Boston King beat his Democratic rival 73 to 27 percent; in Lowell, 54 to 46 percent; in Lynn, 51 to 49 percent; in Fall River, 55 to 45 percent. Dukakis retained his loyal following in those enclaves where professionals predominated: on Beacon Hill he walloped King 80 to 20 percent; Cambridge gave him 72 percent of its ballots; Newton, 74 percent; Amherst, 83 percent.[14]

Although social and cultural issues continue to fracture Massachusetts politics, Edward Moore Kennedy continues to perform the near-Herculean task of uniting Massachusetts Democrats. Kennedy was overwhelmingly endorsed for reelection by delegates to the state convention; he received "excellent" or "pretty good" ratings on his job performance from 94 to 75 percent of the Dukakis and King delegates respectively; and he was supported for the 1984 Democratic presidential nomination by 65 and 70 percent of the King and Dukakis backers.[15] King and Dukakis delegates also agreed with Kennedy's positions on the "unity" issues: 68 and 72 percent supported his plan for national health insurance; 56 and 75 percent believed "too little" is spent by government on "solving the problems of the big cities."[16] One state representative wearing Kennedy and King buttons conveyed the Democrats' dilemma. When asked if the party was "schizoid," he replied, "No, it's just the Democratic party."[17]

The Republicans: Down for the Count?

After the primary Massachusetts Democrats suffered from battle fatigue. Lieutenant Governor Thomas P. O'Neill III put it this way: "The Democratic primary was so spectacular, it was so high-pitched that it drained everybody—drained them emotionally and financially."[18] King and Dukakis, for example, each spent $2.5 million on the primary—most of it for media advertisements.

With the Democrats so exhausted, Republican candidates should have been able to land a few knockout punches. Yet in the election, the GOP suffered a complete rout. On election night former Republican Governor Frank Sargent bemoaned the "disaster."[19] No statewide GOP candidate received more than 39 percent of the vote; the two Republican congressional seats were reduced to one; the party did not contest 55 percent of the seats in the General Court; Republican losses in the state Senate left the party's contingent one vote shy of the eight required to demand a roll call. John Sears, the 1982 Republican nominee for governor, says: "The whole party [is] threatened with the possibility of such weakness that we must either straighten ourselves or die."[20] Ray Shamie, the defeated GOP U.S. Senate candidate, concedes: "In Massachusetts we have a one-party state."[21] Former GOP State Chairman Gordon Nelson opines, "At the grassroots level, the Republican party is in desperately bad shape."[22] Sargent was particularly dispirited:

The party has been on its knees for a long time. [But now] there is nothing there. I can only rationalize and say that maybe it's a good thing that it is dead. . . . Maybe it can somehow be totally reorganized with a different kind of name like Independent-Republican Party.[23]

Whether or not the Republican party in Massachusetts can effect such a total reorganization remains to be seen. But one thing appears certain: it is moribund, and likely to remain that way for years to come.

Rhode Island: An "Upside-Down" Victory

Massachusetts Republicans ought to be envious of their Rhode Island counterparts. There, three prominent GOP candidates bested their Democratic rivals: John Chafee won reelection to the U.S. Senate; Susan Farmer won as secretary of the state, becoming the first Republican to capture that post since 1938; and Republican Congresswoman Claudine Schneider easily defeated Democrat Jim Aukerman by a margin of 56 to 44 percent.[24]

A closer look at the Republican winners, however, underscores the weakness of their party. Rather than playing up their GOP affiliation, each chose to avoid it. The *Hartford Courant* in an article on Chafee's candidacy headlined, "'Mr. Republican' Seeks Party Anonymity."[25] Claudine Schneider's campaign literature also avoided the word "Republican." And in Providence, Republican Mayor Vincent A. Cianci eschewed the party completely by running for reelection as an Independent. Vincent Marzullo, the 1982 GOP gubernatorial nominee, noted that Rhode Island has evolved so completely into a one-party bailiwick "that many Republican candidates don't even use the word 'Republican' in their literature."[26]

The election results affirm Marzullo's assessment. Democratic Governor J. Joseph Garrahy was reelected to a fourth term, capturing 73 percent of the vote and thirty-eight of the thirty-nine cities and towns. Republican Marzullo was so unknown that former U.S.

Senator John O. Pastore could sarcastically boast of Garrahy: "We didn't have to go through the Yellow Pages to find him."[27] Marzullo raised only $20,000 compared with Garrahy's $526,000, prompting the *Providence Journal* to remark that "Marzullo's campaign makes this the closest thing to a forfeit that Rhode Islanders have seen in an election for governor in at least a generation."[28]

Other Rhode Island Democrats fared nearly as well as Garrahy with the nominees for general treasurer, lieutenant governor, and attorney general capturing 78, 60, and 57 percent of the ballots respectively.[29] Democrats increased their control in the Rhode Island House of Representatives with most of the contest decided long before the November election.[30] Republicans chose not to field candidates in nearly half of the representative contests. The election results in Warwick were typical of the GOP weakness. Voters in this large, predominantly white-collar suburb returned incumbent Democratic Mayor Joseph Walsh to city hall for the third time with 87 percent of the vote.[31] Seven of nine Democratic council members were also reelected, two without GOP opposition. In addition, Warwick's only Republican delegate to the General Assembly was defeated for reelection.

The GOP donnybrook did not happen overnight. Twenty years ago the last Republican mayor of Warwick, Raymond Stone, was defeated for reelection. A decade ago the party lost control of the City Council. One discouraged Republican, former Ninth Ward Chairman Armenag Palin, observes: "There is no Republican party in Warwick. . . . Republicans have been eating crumbs off the floor for so long, they wouldn't know how to sit at the table and eat like men."[32]

Thus, at the end of 1982, the chief problem the Democratic party faces in Rhode Island is too many candidates and not enough offices. One Democrat observed, "You've got to open the party up to more people. It's closing in on us. . . . The way things are now there is no room for advancement."[33] A survey of Democrats occupying statewide posts makes the point: Governor Garrahy, Lieutenant Governor Di Luglio, and General Treasurer Solomon are beginning their fourth two-year terms; Claiborne Pell is entering his twenty-second year in the U.S. Senate; and Ferdinand St. Germain is beginning his twelfth term in the U.S. House of Representatives. Should any one of these prominent Democrats step aside an intense squabble would surely ensue that dealt not with substantive issues, but with who might gain a possible long-term promotion. Whatever the outcome, one thing is certain: in the Ocean State the Democratic tide is still running strong.

Connecticut: "What Makes Lowell Weicker Run?"

At first glance 1982 was a commendable year for Connecticut Republicans: Lowell Weicker was reelected to a third term in the U.S. Senate; Republican Nancy Johnson captured a Democratic congressional seat; and the GOP clung to a respectable minority status in the legislature. The state legislature results were particularly encouraging for Republicans. There the party retained thirteen seats in the state Senate and sixty-four seats in the House. These seventy-seven GOP legislators provide a viable "talent base" for the future.

In other races, however, the GOP did not fare as well: it lost the bid for the governorship for the third time since 1970; lost every statewide office—except Weicker's U.S. Senate seat; lost Congressman De Nardis; lost to the remaining incumbent Democratic congressmen. Party registration also continued to favor the Democrats, with the party leading by 225,000.[34]

Yet in those races where Republican candidates were victorious, their party identification played an ancillary role. As Lowell Weicker put it: "Instead of a well-done from your party you get a kick in the tail."[35] Rather than concentrating on the Democrats, Connecticut Republicans spent much of 1982 positioned in a small circle, firing most of their political volleys at each other. Prescott Bush, brother of the vice-president, challenged Weicker at the GOP convention and obtained enough support to force a primary—something he eventually backed away from. But Bush's challenge represented an ongoing fight among Connecticut Republicans for the party's soul. At the forefront of the debate was Pragmatist Lowell Weicker.

First elected to the U.S. Senate in 1970, Weicker had the trappings of an Orthodox Republican. A supporter of Nixon's Vietnam War policy, Weicker promised that there would be a "nice jail cell" waiting for the draft evaders, "not only now, but after the war is over."[36] Then Vice-President Spiro T. Agnew praised Weicker, calling him "a born leader."[37]

Almost as quickly as he was elected, however, Weicker began to defy the party hierarchy. As a member of the Senate Watergate Committee he castigated the tactics of Nixon's 1972 Committee to Re-elect the President. At one point Nixon wondered aloud to aide John Ehrlichman, "What the hell makes Lowell Weicker run?" Ehrlichman responded, "Nobody's been able to figure that out."[38]

Some Connecticut Republicans are still trying. In 1982 he denounced the Reagan budget and tax cuts saying, "God help the United States of America if we have two more years like that."[39] In his acceptance speech at the state convention Weicker flaunted his disobedience of the Reagan administration by citing his efforts to protect Connecticut's minorities and disabled; his advocacy of the Equal Rights Amendment; his opposition to such proposed constitutional amendments as school prayer and busing; his proposal to increase the minimum wage and veteran benefits.[40] Using classic Pragmatist terminology, Weicker contended Connecticut's Republican party needed live bodies, "not dead philosophers":

[We] are not going to be the majority party in this state based on what circumstances are *not*. . . . One-party politics has damned near destroyed the excellence of Connecticut politics. And the only way to rectify this circumstance is to go nose-to-nose with Democrats instead of back-to-back with Republicans. [Emphasis added.][41]

Orthodox Republicans forcefully disagreed with Weicker's views. Prescott Bush promised to be more faithful to the Reagan administration's policies, and Conservative party candidate Lucien Di-Fazio advocated traditional Orthodox policies of laissez faire. When the ballots were counted Weicker had 51 percent; Moffett, 46 percent; DiFazio, 3 percent.[42] Weicker's margin was aided considerably by his appeal to traditional Democratic constituencies. Jewish voters gave him 54 percent of their ballots; blue-collar workers, 45 percent; Catholics, 49 percent.[43] Yet, Weicker's success—like Nancy Johnson's—was personal rather than party oriented. Weicker's slogan, "Nobody's man but yours," boldly proclaimed his independence. During the campaign he insisted that "Connecticut is my party."[44] Loser Toby Moffett summed up Weicker's strategy: "Obviously, he is a very tough customer and he succeeded just brilliantly by portraying himself as a very tough individual who just wasn't beholden to anybody."[45]

Weicker's GOP "divorce" does not bode well for Connecticut Republicans. GOP State Chairman Ralph Capecelatro argues:

If you are a Republican, you should be a Republican day and night, and from week to week. If you are a "sometime Republican," I do not think you are going to be as good a party person. . . . There is such a thing as party loyalty. If we are not going to have that, then there is not much sense in having a Republican party or a Democratic party.[46]

Until Connecticut Republicans resolve their differences, Democrats—to paraphrase R. E. Van Norstrand—will continue to enjoy happy election eves.

APPENDIX

Table 1 Voter Characteristics in Massachusetts, by Party Affiliation, 1980 (in percentages)

	Democrat/ Lean Democrat	Republican/ Lean Republican	Independent
Statewide	58	30	12
Sex			
Male	57	31	12
Female	59	28	12
Race			
White	57	31	12
Black	86	10	4
Education			
Graduate work	61	32	7
College graduate	59	31	10
Some college	52	35	13
High school graduate	58	30	12
Less than high school	63	23	14
Section of State			
Suffolk County	69	18	14
Essex County	54	34	12
Middlesex County	63	27	11
Norfolk County	54	37	10
Southeast	53	36	11
Worcester County	58	27	15
West	56	32	13
Age			
18–29	58	31	11
30–49	59	27	15
50–59	58	31	11
60 and over	56	34	10

Table 1 continued

	Democrat/ Lean Democrat	Republican/ Lean Republican	Independent
Income			
Under $10,000	65	24	10
$10,000–14,999	62	24	13
$15,000–19,999	57	30	13
$20,000–29,999	61	30	9
$30,000 and over	47	43	10
Religion			
Catholic	67	22	11
Protestant	37	51	12
Jewish	74	15	10
Union Membership			
Union	63	27	11
Nonunion	56	32	12

SOURCE: Clark University, Public Affairs Research Center, combined Massachusetts surveys, March and October 1980.
NOTE: Total sample size of combined surveys = 2,010.

Table 2 Characteristics in Connecticut, by Party Affiliation, 1981 and 1982 (in percentages)

	Democrat	Republican	Independent
Statewide	30	25	45
Sex			
Male	27	25	48
Female	33	26	42
Race			
White	29	27	45
Nonwhite	57	5	38
Education			
College graduate	26	30	43
Some college	29	25	45
High school graduate	31	22	47
Less than high school	39	21	39

Table 2 continued

	Democrat	Republican	Independent
Section of State			
Fairfield County	23	37	40
Hartford County	38	21	41
East Connecticut River	34	20	47
Others	28	23	50
Age			
18–29	32	19	49
30–44	29	20	51
45–59	28	34	38
60 and over	33	29	38
Occupation			
Professional and business	26	31	43
White-collar	32	23	44
Blue-collar	33	16	51
Not in workforce	37	28	35
Income			
Under $10,000	37	23	40
$10,000–$14,999	38	15	47
$15,000–$19,999	42	18	41
$20,000–$29,999	29	21	50
$30,000 and over	20	37	43
Religion			
Catholic	39	20	42
Protestant	20	37	42
Other	33	15	52
Union Membership			
Union	32	20	48
Nonunion	30	27	44

SOURCE: University of Connecticut, Institute for Social Inquiry, combined Connecticut polls, December 1981, January and February 1982.
NOTE: Total sample size of combined surveys = 1,500.

Table 3 Voter Characteristics in Rhode Island, by Party Affiliation, 1980 (in percentages)

	Democrat/ Lean Democrat	Republican/ Lean Republican	Independent
Statewide	54	16	25
Sex			
Male	51	19	26
Female	57	13	24
Education			
Some college or graduate	49	25	22
High school graduate	54	16	25
High school incomplete	56	13	27
Eighth grade or less	60	8	25
County			
Providence	57	12	26
Bristol	54	25	15
Newport	55	19	25
Kent	47	21	23
Washington	52	17	27
Age			
18–29	61	20	15
30–39	55	18	24
40–49	49	11	36
50–59	49	15	31
60 and over	55	12	26

SOURCE: Opinion Research Corporation (Princeton, N.J.) survey, 15–18 February 1980.
NOTE: Total sample size = 1,007.
NOTE: Percentages are weighted.

Table 4 Democratic Presidential Vote in Massachusetts, Rhode Island, and Connecticut Counties Voting Republican in 1960, 1960–1980 (in percentages)

County	1960	1964	1968	1972	1976	1980
Massachusetts:						
Barnstable	37	57	39	38	44	29
Dukes	39	68	48	46	52	45
Franklin	44	67	48	43	50	40
Nantucket	36	67	42	40	44	37
Plymouth	48	68	53	48	53	34
Rhode Island:						
Washington	48	71	52	41	50	41
Connecticut						
Fairfield	47	61	42	35	42	34
Litchfield	46	66	46	39	44	35
Tolland	49	69	49	43	49	37

SOURCES: Massachusetts Secretary of the Commonwealth, *Massachusetts Election Statistics, 1960–1980*, Public Document, No. 43 (Boston, 1980); *Manual for the General Assembly of Rhode Island, 1960–1961* through *1980–1981*; *Connecticut Register and Manual, 1961* through *1981*.

Table 5 Voter Characteristics in the United States, by Party Affiliation, 1981 (in percentages)

	Republican	Democratic	Independent
National	28	41	31
Sex			
Male	28	38	34
Female	28	44	28
Race			
White	30	37	33
Black	8	75	17
Other	13	48	33
Region			
East	28	41	31
Midwest	29	36	35
South	25	46	29
West	31	41	28
Education			
College	35	32	33
High school	27	41	32
Grade school	19	59	22

Table 5 continued

	Republican	Democratic	Independent
Age			
18–24	26	34	40
25–29	22	38	40
30–49	27	40	33
50 and older	31	47	22
Income			
Under $5,000	20	55	25
$ 5,000– 9,999	23	48	29
$10,000–14,999	24	45	31
$15,000–19,999	27	41	32
$20,000–24,999	29	38	33
$25,000 and over	35	33	32
Religion			
Protestant	32	40	28
Catholic	23	45	32
Jewish	16	55	29
Other	18	36	46
Occupation			
Professional and business	35	32	33
Clerical and sales	25	43	32
Manual workers	22	44	34
Farmers	44	27	29
Nonlabor force	29	49	22
City Size			
1,000,000 and over	25	46	29
500,000–999,999	24	41	35
50,000–499,999	26	42	32
2,500–49,999	27	42	31
Under 2,500 rural	33	38	29
Union Membership			
Union families	21	48	31
Nonunion families	30	39	31

SOURCE: *Gallup Report*, no. 187, April 1981, p. 22.

NOTES

Preface

1. *Public Opinion*, June/July 1980, pp. 21, 28.
2. Ibid., p. 24.
3. Ibid., p. 22.
4. Clinton Rossiter, *Parties and Politics in America* (Ithaca, N.Y.: Cornell University Press, 1960), pp. 12, 13.
5. V. O. Key, Jr., *American State Politics: An Introduction* (New York: Alfred A. Knopf, 1965), p. v.

Introduction

1. Harold D. Lasswell, *Politics: Who Gets What, When, How* (New York: Meridian Books, 1958).
2. Samuel Lubell, *The Future of American Politics*, 3d ed. (New York: Harper & Row, 1965), p. 195.
3. James Russell Lowell, "New England Two Centuries Ago," *Literary Essays*, vol. 2 (Boston: Houghton Mifflin, 1890), p. 8.
4. Nathan Glazer and Daniel Patrick Moynihan, *Beyond the Melting Pot: The Negroes, Puerto Ricans, Jews, Italians and Irish of New York City*, 2d ed. (Cambridge, Mass.: MIT Press, 1970), p. 222.
5. "Polarizing the Nation?" *Newsweek*, 8 February 1982. To the question "Do you think federal spending in the following areas should be cut further, increased, or remain the same?" respondents supported increasing or maintaining the same level of spending in the following proportions: medical and health care, 86 percent; job training, 84 percent; protecting the environment, 81 percent; aid to education/college loans, 79 percent; aid to the states and cities, 75 percent; farm price supports, 65 percent; food stamps, 53 percent; and welfare, 52 percent.
6. American Institute of Public Opinion (Gallup Poll), surveys 624 (4–9

February 1960) and 662 (23–28 August 1962); University of Chicago, National Opinion Research Center, General Social Survey, 1978.

Chapter 1

1. Neal R. Peirce, *The New England States: People, Politics, and Power in the Six New England States* (New York: W. W. Norton, 1976), p. 64.

2. Daniel Chauncey Brewer, *The Conquest of New England by the Immigrant* (New York: G. P. Putnam and Sons, 1926), p. 120.

3. Rhode Island, *Census* (Providence, State of Rhode Island, 1865). Rhode Island and Massachusetts conducted decennial censuses throughout the nineteenth century.

4. Joseph I. Lieberman, *The Power Broker: A Biography of John M. Bailey, Modern Political Boss* (Boston: Houghton Mifflin, 1966), p. 22.

5. U.S. Department of Commerce, Bureau of the Census, *Historical Statistics of the United States: Colonial Times to 1970.* (Washington, D.C., 1975), pp. 105–06.

6. The Rhode Island Twenty-third Representative District.

7. Brewer, *The Conquest of New England by the Immigrant.*

8. In this discussion, *Protestants* means white Protestants specifically. New England blacks, who are also largely Protestant, had joined the ranks of the Democratic party by the end of the 1930s. Blacks currently constitute a small part of the southern New England electorate: Massachusetts, 4 percent; Connecticut, 7 percent; Rhode Island, 3 percent. Source: Michael Barone and Grant Ujifusa, *The Almanac of American Politics, 1982* (Washington, D.C.: Barone and Company, 1981), pp. 183, 488, 992. The tensions between white Protestants and Catholics remained the most important factor in determining the political agenda of the region.

9. Duane Lockard, *New England State Politics* (Princeton: Princeton University Press, 1959), pp. 305–7.

10. Richard A. Gabriel, *The Political Machine in Rhode Island* (Kingston: University of Rhode Island, Bureau of Government Research, 1970), p. 5. In 1928 the property qualification was removed and voter registration increased greatly. The 1901 Rhode Island Brayton Law was another attempt to forestall the effects of the rising number of Catholic voters. Realizing that the Catholic-dominated Democratic party might win the governorship more often in the twentieth century, Republican boss Charles R. Brayton pushed through legislation stripping the governor of all appointive power and vesting it in the Republican-dominated state Senate. Under this law, if the Senate did not confirm gubernatorial appointments within three days, it could designate its own choices for the positions.

11. Everett Carll Ladd, *American Political Parties: Social Change and Political Response* (New York: W. W. Norton, 1970), p. 146.

12. "A Law with Fangs," editorial in the *Providence Visitor*, 19 September 1924; and "The Aim," editorial, ibid., 24 April 1924, p. 4.

13. The term *Catholic collectivity* also included the Jews. Though not bulking large in the total state populations, Jews were a sizable bloc in certain districts in the large cities. Jewish voters eventually sided with Catholics on most major ethnocultural and economic issues.

14. Massachusetts Democratic Party, *State Platform*, 1913 and Massachusetts Republican Party, *State Platform*, 1913.

15. Connecticut Democratic Party, *State Platform*, 1928.

16. "Rhode Island Democrats Take a Wringing Wet Stand, Call for Destruction of GOP Machine," *Providence Journal*, 2 October 1930, p. 6.

17. Massachusetts Democratic Party, *State Platform*, 1910.

18. Connecticut Democratic Party, *State Platform*, 1920.

19. Connecticut Democratic Party, *State Platform*, 1924.

20. Figures for the period are drawn from *State of Connecticut Register and Manual, 1900* through *1928* (Hartford: State of Connecticut, 1901–1928) (hereafter cited as *Connecticut Register and Manual*); Massachusetts General Court, *A Manual for the Use of the General Court, 1900* through *1927–1928* (Boston, 1901–1929) (hereafter cited as *Manual for the General Court*); and Rhode Island General Assembly, *Manual with Rules and Orders for the Use of the General Assembly of the State of Rhode Island, 1901–1902* through *1927–1928* (Providence, 1902–1928) (hereafter cited as *Manual for General Assembly of Rhode Island*). Four measures are employed: (1) the average percentage of the popular vote won by Democratic gubernatorial candidates; (2) the average percentage of seats in the state Senates controlled by the Democrats; (3) the mean percentage of seats in the state Houses of Representatives held by the Democrats; (4) the percentage of all the gubernatorial and state legislative terms controlled by the Democrats. The four percentages are averaged to produce an index of competitiveness, with zero representing total Republican success and one signifying complete Democratic success.

21. Edward M. Kennedy to the author, 24 January 1983.

22. Edgar Litt, *The Political Cultures of Massachusetts* (Cambridge, Mass.: MIT Press, 1965), p. 34.

23. Quoted in J. Joseph Huthmacher, *Massachusetts: People and Politics, 1919–1933* (New York: Atheneum, 1969), p. 154.

24. According to Richard Hofstader, "There was not a Democrat alive, Protestant or Catholic, who could have beaten Hoover in 1928"; quoted in David Burner, *The Politics of Provincialism: The Democratic Party in Transition, 1918–1932* (New York: Alfred A. Knopf, 1968), p. 180. Ruth Silva has also concluded that Smith's membership in the Democratic party was his greatest liability; Ruth Silva, *Rum, Religion, and Votes: 1928 Re-examined* (University Park, Pa.: State University Press, 1962).

25. Boston's Second Ward, Providence's Eighth Representative District, and Hartford's Ninth Ward. The records of Providence's ward returns for 1928 were irreparably damaged during Hurricane Carol in 1953. The only

returns now available are those for the representative districts, published in the *Providence Journal Almanac.*

26. Boston's First Ward, Providence's Fourteenth Representative District, and Hartford's Second Ward.

27. A rural Yankee town is defined as one with a population of 3,500 or less and having 60 percent or more native whites, based on the figures of the 1930 Census (U.S. Department of Commerce, Bureau of the Census, *Fifteenth Census of the United States: 1930* [Washington, D.C.]). Twenty-one towns in Connecticut, eight in Rhode Island, and eighty-one in Massachusetts met these criteria.

28. Huthmacher, *Massachusetts*, p. 162.

29. "Boston Gives Heart to Smith: Greeting Breaks All Records," *Boston Evening Globe*, 24 October 1928, p. 1.

30. Alfred E. Smith, *Up to Now: An Autobiography* (New York: Viking Press, 1929), p. 403.

31. "Thousands Acclaim Smith in Hartford's Greatest of Ovations," *Hartford Courant*, 25 October 1928, p. 1.

32. "Al Smith Acclaimed by Thousands on Trip to Providence," *Providence Journal*, 26 October 1928, p. 1.

33. According to Samuel Lubell, the Second World War had a substantial impact on the voting behavior of virtually all ethnic groups within the Democratic coalition. Italians, smarting over U.S. actions against Mussolini, were not as faithful in 1944 as before. The Irish also responded negatively to Roosevelt's wartime intervention on behalf of the British. See Samuel Lubell, *The Future of American Politics*, 3d ed. (New York: Harper & Row, 1965), especially pp. 202–04.

34. Providence's Fourteenth Representative District, Boston's First Ward, Hartford's Second Ward.

35. Boston's Second Ward, Providence's Eighth Representative District, and Hartford's Ninth Ward.

36. Interview with John Chafee, Washington, D.C., 19 October 1979.

37. Connecticut Republican Party, *State Platform*, 1936.

38. "GOP Platform Assails Democratic Dual Office Holding, Pledges to End Practice," *Providence Journal*, 8 October 1936.

39. Connecticut Republican Party, *State Platform*, 1936.

40. Connecticut Republican Party, *State Platform*, 1934.

41. This electoral victory was popularly known in Rhode Island as the "Green Revolution." Democrat Theodore Francis Green won the 1932 and 1934 gubernatorial contests, but the hands of the Democrats were securely tied during his first term by Republican control of the General Assembly. The Republican position was strengthened by the Brayton Law (see note 10, above). Thus, the state was in the unusual position of having a Democrat as governor and Republicans in nearly all other administrative and judicial positions.

In 1934 the Rhode Island House of Representatives passed into Democratic hands and the Republicans appeared to have a two-seat majority in the Senate. When the latter convened, the Democratic lieutenant governor refused to swear in two closely elected GOP senators. A committee was appointed to recount the ballots in the two contests and, predictably, the Democratic candidates received pluralities—ten and twenty-four votes. With the Senate newly Democratic, effective control of the state government passed from Republican hands. Many Republican appointees were ousted; several boards and commissions were abolished; and the state's Supreme Court justices, Republicans all, were removed.

42. "Democrats Adopt State Platform," *Providence Journal*, 7 October 1936, p. 7.

43. The information on the origins of Connecticut's state treasurers is from Lockard, *New England State Politics*, p. 238. The current treasurer, Henry E. Parker, is a black. Information on the ethnicity of Rhode Island congressmen is from David D. Warren, "Hyphenated Americanism in Rhode Island Politics," *Alumni Bulletin of the University of Rhode Island* 3 (October 1964): 3. Republican Claudine Schneider ousted Irish Democrat Edward P. Beard in Rhode Island's Second Congressional District in 1980.

44. Interview with John O. Pastore, Providence, 24 October 1979.

45. See Elmer Cornwell, "Rhode Island: The Long Count and Its Aftermath," in *Party Politics in the New England States*, ed. George Goodwin, Jr., and Victoria Schuck (Durham, N.H.: New England Center for Continuing Education, 1968); Lockard, *New England State Politics*, pp. 193–95.

46. University of Connecticut, Institute for Social Inquiry, combined Connecticut polls, December 1981, January and February 1982.

47. Clark University, Public Affairs Research Center, Massachusetts survey, October 1978.

48. Everett Carll Ladd with Charles D. Hadley, *Transformations of the American Party System: Political Coalitions from the New Deal to the 1970s* (New York: W. W. Norton, 1978), p. 298.

49. "For Many Catholics in America, Respect Is an Elusive Prize," *Boston Globe*, 4 February 1979, p. 1.

50. Clark University, Public Affairs Research Center, combined Massachusetts surveys, October 1978 and February 1979.

51. University of Connecticut, Institute for Social Inquiry, combined Connecticut polls, March, August, November, and December 1979.

52. Clark University, Public Affairs Research Center, Massachusetts survey, February 1979. Text of the question: "Should more money, less money, or the same amount of money be spent on welfare?" The Protestant response includes whites only.

53. University of Connecticut, Institute for Social Inquiry, combined Connecticut polls, March, August, November, and December 1979.

54. Interview with Ronald Civins-Mills, Providence, 25 October 1979.

55. Interview with Claiborne Pell, Washington, D.C., 19 October 1979.

56. Interview with Francis W. Sargent, Boston, 24 October 1979.

57. Interview with Michael S. Dukakis, Cambridge, 30 October 1979. Greek Americans account for less than one percent of the Massachusetts population.

58. Clark University, Public Affairs Research Center, Massachusetts survey, March 1979. Text of the question: "Think of a situation in which there are three candidates running for governor of Massachusetts. One is a Protestant Yankee; one is Irish Catholic; and one is an Italian Catholic. Which of these three would you be *least* likely to vote for—the Protestant Yankee, the Irish Catholic, or the Italian Catholic?"

59. Wards Three, Nine, Eleven, and Twelve are Irish; Wards Four, Seven, and Thirteen are Italian. The remaining wards (One, Two, Five, Six, Eight, and Ten) are construed as being ethnically mixed. The classifications were made by Richard A. Gabriel, *Ethnic Voting in Primary Elections: The Case of Providence, Rhode Island* (Kingston: University of Rhode Island, Bureau of Government Research, 1969), p. 10.

60. Ethnic loyalties played a greater role in the 1978 mayoral election. Cianci easily defeated his Irish Catholic Democratic opponent by almost two to one in the Italian wards, but the Democratic candidate won a small majority in the Irish wards, 51 to 49 percent. Cianci's impressive majority in the Italian wards may be attributed in part to the weakness of his opponent rather than to his Italian heritage.

61. NBC News, primary day survey, September 1978.

62. American Institute of Public Opinion, Surveys 642 (2 February 1960), 666 (2 August 1962), 721 (9 December 1965), and 764 (24 June 1968); and University of Chicago, National Opinion Research Center, general social survey, 1972–1978, cumulative.

63. University of Chicago, National Opinion Research Center, general social surveys, 1972–1978, cumulative. NORC data are for New England as a region; there are few good state data on these issues. The surveys of southern New England that do exist show the same trends.

64. Clark University, Public Affairs Research Center, Massachusetts survey, March 1979.

65. Author's tape recording of Massachusetts gubernatorial candidates' debate, Boston, 31 August 1978.

66. Clark University, Public Affairs Research Center, Massachusetts survey, October 1978.

67. In 1980, Boston's Cardinal Humberto Medeiros in a strongly worded letter described abortion as "an unspeakable crime" and said that "those who make abortions possible by law—such as legislators and those who promote, defend, and elect those same lawmakers—cannot segregate themselves totally from that guilt which accompanies this horrendous crime and deadly sin"; "Fifty-Five Clerics Protest Distorted Actions on Frank," *Bos-*

ton Sunday Globe, 14 September 1980. The cardinal's letter was viewed as a plea to voters in the Fourth Congressional District not to vote for Democratic candidate Barney Frank, a Jew, in the congressional primary. The Fourth District is a highly educated and largely Catholic area. The district's previous congressman was Father Robert Drinan, S.J., a Democrat. The cardinal's letter had little effect on the vote: Frank won the primary with 52 percent; his antiabortion opponent received 47 percent.

Chapter 2

1. For an interesting discussion of this point see John S. Hekman and John S. Strong, "The Evolution of New England Industry," *New England Economic Review,* March/April 1981, pp. 35–46.

2. John S. Hekman, "What Attracts Industry to New England?" *New England Economic Indicators,* December 1978, p. A3.

3. Federal Reserve Bank of Boston, *New England at Work in the Space Age: 1961 Annual Report* (Boston, 1961), p. 9.

4. Interview with Warren A. Johnson, Boston, 1 November 1979.

5. Jane Jacobs, *The Economy of Cities* (New York: Random House, 1969), p. 203.

6. U.S. Department of Labor, Bureau of Labor Statistics, *The Changing Structure of New England Employment, 1947–1973* (Washington, D.C., 1973), pp. 3–4.

7. Ibid., p. 3; "Massachusetts Still Filling Vacuum Left by Shoe, Textile Shutdowns," *Boston Globe,* 26 March 1973, p. 1.

8. Department of Labor, *Changing Structure of New England Employment,* p. 3.

9. Interview with James M. Howell, Boston, 8 January 1982.

10. Woodrow Wilson International Center for Scholars, *Prospects for New England; Highlights of Proceedings and Supplementary Papers from a Conference at the Woodrow Wilson International Center for Scholars,* October 7, 1974 (Washington, D.C., 1974), pp. 18–19.

11. Figures supplied by the Massachusetts Division of Employment Security, Research Division.

12. See Daniel Bell, *The Coming of Post-Industrial Society* (New York: Basic Books, 1973); Zbigniew Brzezinski, *Between Two Ages: America's Role in the Technetronic Era* (New York: Viking Press, 1970).

13. Radovan Richta, *Civilization at the Crossroads: Social and Human Implications of the Scientific and Technological Revolution* (Prague, Czechoslovakia: International Arts and Sciences Press, 1969), p. 43.

14. U.S. Department of Commerce, Bureau of the Census, *Statistical Abstract of the United States, 1979* (Washington, D.C., 1979), p. 160; idem, *Historical Statistics of the United States: Colonial Times to 1970* (Washington, D.C., 1975), p. 383.

15. For the 1940s figures, see Daniel Bell, "The New Class: A Muddled Concept," in *The New Class?* ed. B. Bruce Briggs (New Brunswick, N.J.: Transaction Books, 1979), p. 178. For the 1975 figures, see Michael Harrington, "The New Class and the Left," in *The New Class?* p. 128.

16. Bell, *Post-Industrial Society*, p. 220.

17. James E. McCarthy, *Trade and Adjustment Assistance: A Case Study of the Shoe Industry in Massachusetts*, Research Report No. 58 (Boston: Federal Reserve Bank of Boston, 1975), p. 42.

18. U.S. Department of Commerce, Bureau of the Census, *The Sixteenth Census of the United States: 1940* (Washington, D.C., 1943); idem, *The Nineteenth Decennial Census of the United States. Census of Population: 1970* (Washington, D.C., 1972).

19. Department of Commerce, *Sixteenth Census, 1940*.

20. Hekman and Strong, "Evolution of New England Industry," p. 42.

21. "Technology: Alchemist of Route 128," *New York Times*, 8 January 1968, p. 139.

22. "New England: What Replaces Old Industry?," *Business Week*, 4 August 1973, p. 39.

23. Digital Equipment Corporation, *Annual Report, 1981* (Maynard, Mass., 1982).

24. Ann Bristow, "American Survey: New England," *London Economist*, 9 May 1981, p. 56.

25. Digital, *Annual Report, 1981*.

26. Interview with James Howell, Boston, 16 January 1980.

27. Data General, *1981 Annual Report* (Westboro, Mass., 1982), p. 1.

28. "State of Opportunity: Massachusetts Is Loaded with Good Investment Opportunities," *Boston Globe*, 27 January 1980, p. 61.

29. Figures supplied by Massachusetts Department of Commerce and Economic Development.

30. See Massachusetts Department of Commerce and Economic Development, *Comprehensive Cost Profile High-Technology Electronics Manufacturing* (Boston, 1978), p. 6.

31. Figures derived from New England Board of Higher Education, *Facts about New England Colleges, Universities, and Institutes, 1977–1978* (Wellesley, Mass., 1978).

32. Interview with Howell, 8 January 1982.

33. "Keeping Up with Youth," *Parade Magazine*, 18 March 1979, p. 17.

34. Massachusetts Department of Commerce, *High-Technology Electronics Manufacturing*, p. 9.

35. Interview with Ray Stata, Norwood, Mass., 6 December 1979.

36. "Head Man at Digital Family Man at Heart," *Boston Globe*, 2 April 1973; Elizabeth P. Deutermann, "Seeding Science-Based Industry," *New England Business Review*, December 1966, p. 7.

37. Everett J. Burtt, Jr., *Influence of Labor Supply on Location of Elec-*

tronics Firms, Research Report No. 34 (Boston: Federal Reserve Bank of Boston, 1966), p. 20.

38. Interview with Stata.

39. Massachusetts Department of Commerce, *High-Technology Electronics Manufacturing*, p. 28.

40. "Research Firm to Concentrate on Route 128 Site," *Boston Globe*, 12 February 1972, p. 3.

41. "Two Bay State Minicomputer Firms See Expansion Ahead," *Boston Globe*, 2 April 1973, p. 1.

42. Data derived from Massachusetts Department of Commerce and Development, first quarter 1978; and Connecticut Labor Department, Employment Security Division, June 1977.

43. "MIT to Study Science Impact," *Boston Globe*, 4 June 1978.

44. "Technology: Alchemist of Route 128."

45. "We've Been Begging for People . . . ," *Boston Globe*, 27 January 1980.

46. Massachusetts Institute of Technology, Industrial Liaison Program brochure, p. 14.

47. Peter H. McCormick to author, 26 February 1979.

48. Interview with Johnson, 1 November 1979.

49. Seymour Martin Lipset, "The New Class and the Professoriate," in *The New Class?* pp. 72–73.

50. Massachusetts Occupation Industry Research Department, Research and Information Service, *Employment Requirements for Massachusetts by Occupation, by Industry, 1970–1974–1985* (Boston, 1976), p. 15.

51. Ibid.

52. Interview with Stata.

53. "Technology: Alchemist of Route 128," p. 139.

54. "Routes 128 and 495: Problem and Promise," *Boston Globe*, 14 March 1971, p. 48.

55. Interview with Chester G. Atkins, Boston, 6 January 1982.

56. Ibid.

57. Interview with Michael S. Dukakis, Cambridge, 30 October 1979.

58. "Heckler Receives First-Hand Data About High Tech," *Boston Globe*, 25 November 1981, p. 39.

59. Interview with Johnson, 28 December 1981.

60. Edward Stockton, "Commissioner Pursues Activist Role," *Hartford Courant*, 28 January 1979, p. 1B.

61. Joel B. Alvord, "Economy Resilient, Says Banker from City," *Hartford Courant*, 28 January 1979, p. 12G.

62. "UTC Continues Acquisitions, Defense Orders," *Hartford Courant*, 27 January 1980, p. 11H.

63. Sales figures are from United Technologies Corporation, *Fulfilling the Promise of Technology: Annual Report for 1978* (Hartford, 1979); infor-

mation on United Technologies' impact on the Connecticut economy is from "Research, Development Important to State's Largest Employer," *Hartford Courant*, 28 January 1979, p. 18G.

64. Dick Davies, "Business: Cautious Optimism," *Connecticut Magazine*, January 1982, p. 102.

65. "Firm's Branch to Serve Connecticut Business Giants," *New York Times*, 21 March 1978, p. 37.

66. "New England: What Replaces Old Industry?," p. 41.

67. Interview with Arthur J. Lumsden, Hartford, 16 October 1979.

68. Connecticut Department of Commerce, *1978 Market Data: Connecticut* (Hartford, 1978), p. 71; Department of Commerce, *Sixteenth Census, 1940*.

69. Interview with Lumsden.

70. "New England: What Replaces Old Industry?," p. 38.

71. Interview with Howell, 8 January 1982.

72. Rhode Island Department of Economic Development, *Rhode Island: Basic Statistics, 1979–1980* (Providence, 1981), p. 24.

73. Interview with Philip W. Noel, Providence, 24 October 1979.

74. Rhode Island, Department of Economic Development, *Rhode Island: Basic Statistics, 1977–1978* (Providence, 1979), p. 106; idem, *Basic Statistics, 1979–1980* (Providence, 1981), p. 104.

75. "For Thousands, a Life in the Shops Means Low Pay and Poor Health," *Providence Journal*, 21 June 1981. This article was part of an in-depth six-part series on the state's jewelry industry.

76. Ibid.

77. Interview with J. Joseph Garrahy, Providence, 6 November 1979.

78. Interview with John O. Pastore, Providence, Rhode Island, 24 October 1979.

79. Interview with Johnson, 28 December 1981.

80. Project Rhode Island, *The Rhode Island Economy: A Plan for the Future* (Providence, 1972), p. 14.

81. "Bills Research Axis Would Aid Economy," *Providence Journal*, 25 March 1965, 16.

82. Project Rhode Island, *The Rhode Island Economy*, p. 21.

83. "State Must Dispel Pro-Labor Image Study Shows," *Providence Journal*, 13 June 1976, p. F1.

84. Interview with Johnson, 1 November 1979.

85. Interview with Georgina MacDonald, Providence, 3 August 1982.

86. Interview with Erskine N. White, Providence, 21 October 1979.

87. Interview with Johnson, 28 December 1981.

88. The data presented in this paragraph are from the University of Chicago, National Opinion Research Center, general social surveys, 1972–1978, cumulative (Chicago: University of Chicago, July 1978).

89. College-educated and non-college-educated respondents differed in their opposition to abortion, 34 and 65 percent, respectively; in support of

the death penalty 49 and 69 percent; and in disapproval of homosexual relationships, 50 and 62 percent. Eighty-four percent of non-college-educated persons believed in the Bible "as the inspired word of God," compared with 57 percent of the college-educated; 48 and 51 percent, respectively, disagreed that women whose husbands have jobs should be laid off first; 51 and 63 percent, respectively, felt that "personal satisfaction and pleasure" were more important than "working hard and doing what is expected"; and 46 and 55 percent, respectively, held that "cleaning up the air" was more important than "preserving jobs"; University of Connecticut, Institute for Social Inquiry, Connecticut polls, November and December 1979, February 1981.

90. Data on all these issues are from Clark University, Public Affairs Research Center, Massachusetts surveys, October 1978 and March 1979.

91. Ibid., October 1978.

92. Bell, "The New Class: A Muddled Concept," p. 186.

93. Quoted in David S. Broder, *The Party's Over: The Failure of Politics in America* (New York: Harper & Row, 1972), p. 111.

94. Quoted in Bell, "The New Class: A Muddled Concept," p. 170.

95. The term is Lionel Trilling's, in *Beyond Culture* (New York: Harcourt Brace Jovanovich, 1978), pp. xii, xiii, xv, xvi.

96. Lipset, "The New Class and the Professoriate," in *The New Class?* p. 70.

97. Richta, *Civilization at the Crossroads*, p. 143.

98. "Proceedings of the State Conference on Immigration in Massachusetts Industries," *Bulletin of the Department of Education* (Massachusetts: 5 November 1920).

99. In 1948 Mansfield, Connecticut, the site of the University of Connecticut; Amherst, Massachusetts, the home of the University of Massachusetts; and Providence Rhode Island's Second Representative District, which then contained Brown University, gave Truman 31, 29, and 33 percent of their votes respectively. In 1972 Mansfield cast 59 percent of its ballots for McGovern; Amherst, 69 percent; and Providence's Third Representative District (which today contains Brown University), 65 percent. *Connecticut Register and Manual, 1949, 1961–1980; Manual for the General Court, 1949–1950, 1961–1962* through *1977–1981*; and State of Rhode Island and Providence Plantations, Board of Elections, *Official Count of the Ballots Cast at the Election* (Providence, 1980).

100. Figures for the period 1966–1980 are from the *Connecticut Register and Manual; Manual for the General Court*, and *Manual for the General Assembly of Rhode Island.* See ch. 1, n. 20 for the measures and methods of computation used.

101. U.S. Department of the Interior, *Statistics of Manufacturers, 1890: City of Newton, Massachusetts*, Census Bulletin No. 342 (Washington, D.C., 1893).

102. "An Affluent Community of 91,000 Starts Its Second 100 Years," *Boston Globe*, 7 May 1973, p. 18.

103. *Directory of New England Manufacturers, 1978* (New York: State Industrial Directories Corporation, 1978); and *Massachusetts State Industrial Directory* (New York: State Industrial Directories Corporation, 1977).

104. Connecticut Development Commission, Research and Information Division, *Community Monographs: East Hartford, Connecticut, 1970* (Hartford, 1970), p. 8.

105. Quoted in East Hartford Chamber of Commerce, "Do You Know Your Own Home Town?" in *East Hartford . . . Paved for Progress* (East Hartford, Conn., 1957).

106. Lee Paquette, *Only More So: The History of East Hartford, 1783–1976* (East Hartford, Conn.: Raymond Library, 1976), p. 116.

107. "Pratt and Whitney Major Factor in Growth of Town," *Hartford Times*, 20 March 1954, p. 1.

108. Robert E. Weiss, Public Relations Department, Pratt and Whitney Aircraft Division to author, 10 April 1979.

109. *Directory of New England Manufacturers, 1978.*

110. Paquette, *Only More So*, p. 314.

111. Connecticut Development Commission, *Community Monographs: East Hartford, 1970*; Paquette, *Only More So*, p. 314.

112. "A Friendly City, Yet—," *Providence Evening Bulletin*, 4 March 1970, p. 1.

113. Rhode Island Historical Preservation Commission, *Central Falls, Rhode Island: Statewide Historical Preservation Report* (Providence, 1978), p. 9.

114. Ibid., p. 40.

115. Ibid., p. 44.

116. "City's Pastime? It Is Politics," *Providence Evening Bulletin*, 4 March 1970, p. 1.

117. Rhode Island Department of Economic Development, *City and Town Monographs, Central Falls: Rhode Island* (Providence, 1976), pp. 5–6.

118. U.S. Department of Commerce, *Nineteenth Decennial Census, 1970.*

119. The figure, from the Rhode Island Department of Employment Security, includes Central Falls, Cumberland, Pawtucket, and Lincoln.

120. Although voter registration in Rhode Island is not by party, election data suggest strong support for the Democratic party given the preference expressed for its candidates.

121. To qualify under the Connecticut challenge primary statute, a candidate must have obtained 20 percent of the votes in any convention roll-call vote and must submit to the secretary of state 5,000 valid signatures of voters enrolled in the same party.

Chapter 3

1. The term is Everett Ladd's. See Everett Carll Ladd, *Where Have All the Voters Gone?* (New York: W. W. Norton, 1978), especially pp. 32–34. Although Republican identifiers are still a significant if dwindling proportion of the electorate, the Democrats enjoy an unprecedented advantage.

2. In 1960 voter registration in Massachusetts was: Democratic, 808,319; Republican, 657,774; and unenrolled, 1,254,266. In 1980 it was: Democratic, 1,368,713; Republican, 453,838; and unenrolled, 1,140,916. In 1960 registration in Connecticut was: Democratic, 360,363; Republican, 359,162; and unaffiliated, 473,727. In 1980 it was: Democratic, 669,131; Republican 449,548; and unaffiliated, 586,660. Rhode Island voters do not state their party preference when registering.

3. Interview with then Governor Ella T. Grasso, Hartford, 16 October 1979.

4. Reapportionment has contributed to the Democratic gains. Before 1962, the Republicans always controlled at least one house of the General Assembly in both Connecticut and Rhode Island. At that time the Connecticut constitution allowed fewer than one-tenth of the voters to elect half of the representatives, and in Rhode Island less than one-fifth of the voters elected a majority of senators. The heavily weighted rural vote virtually assured Republicans control of at least one branch of state government. In 1962 the U.S. Supreme Court ended this arrangement when it ruled that legislative districting was a justiciable matter.

5. Interview with Frederick K. Biebel, Hartford, 17 October 1979.

6. Jack Zaiman, "GOP Outlook Bleak or Worse," *Hartford Courant*, 13 November 1978, p. 18.

7. Interview with John O. Pastore, Providence, 24 October 1979.

8. Interview with John A. Holmes, Jr., Providence, 8 July 1981.

9. Interview with Christopher J. Dodd, Washington, D.C., 19 October 1979.

10. "Connell Behind in Funds Race," *Hartford Courant*, 2 November 1978, p. 51.

11. The Old Confederacy includes Alabama, Georgia, Texas, Mississippi, Louisiana, South Carolina, North Carolina, Tennessee, Virginia, Arkansas, and Florida.

12. This and the following comparative Democratic rankings nationwide are from Richard M. Scammon, *America at the Polls: The Vote for President, 1920–1964* (Pittsburgh: University of Pittsburgh Press, 1965; idem, *America Votes*, vols. 4–11 (Pittsburgh: University of Pittsburgh Press, 1962, 1964, 1966, 1968, 1970, 1972, 1973, 1975); idem and Alice V. McGillivray, *America Votes*, vols. 12–13 (Washington, D.C.: Congressional Quarterly, 1977, 1979).

13. See Everett C. Ladd with Charles D. Hadley, *Transformations of the*

American Party System, 2d ed. (New York: W. W. Norton, 1978), especially chapter 6, "On the 1976 Elections."

14. See Howard Reiter, "Carter's Catholic Problem, or Why Ford Carried Connecticut (and Other Bailiwicks)" (Paper presented at the annual meeting of the Northeastern Political Science Association, Mount Pocono, Pa., 11 November 1977).

15. Anderson received his largest percentage of votes in the following states: Massachusetts, 15.4 percent; Vermont, 15.3; Rhode Island, 14.5; New Hampshire, 13.0; Connecticut, 12.2; Colorado, 11.4; Washington, 11.0; Hawaii, 10.7; Maine, 10.4; and Oregon, 9.8 percent.

16. "Election '80 in Connecticut: A Special Report on the Connecticut Poll Pre-election Survey," University of Connecticut, Institute for Social Inquiry, 3 November 1980.

17. Telephone interview with R. E. Van Norstrand, 20 January 1981.

18. Clark University, Public Affairs Research Center, combined Massachusetts surveys, March and October 1980; University of Connecticut, Institute for Social Inquiry, combined Connecticut polls, December 1981, January and February 1982; Opinion Research Corporation, Rhode Island survey, February 1980.

19. U.S. Department of Commerce, Bureau of the Census, *The Nineteenth Decennial Census of the United States, Census of Population: 1970* (Washington, D.C., 1972).

20. Ibid.

21. In the Connecticut towns with a population of 10,000 to 50,000, McGovern was 35 percentage points behind Kennedy's showing in communities with no residents who had attended college; only when the proportion of those with college exposure reached 18.28 percent did the gap narrow to zero; Office of the Secretary of State in Connecticut.

In the 117 comparable Massachusetts towns, the initial gap of 12 percent narrowed to zero when 18.12 percent of the population had attended college; Massachusetts Secretary of the Commonwealth, *Massachusetts Election Statistics, 1960–1980,* Public Document No. 43 (Boston, 1981). In the 19 Rhode Island towns, an initial gap of 32 percent narrowed to zero when 18.1 percent of residents had college exposure; *Manual for the General Assembly of Rhode Island, 1961* and *1977.* Population statistics are from Department of Commerce, *Nineteenth Decennial Census, 1970.*

22. "Duffey Soft Pedaled Peace," *New York Times,* 20 August 1970, p. 41.

23. James Q. Wilson, *The Amateur Democrat: Club Politics in Three Cities* (Chicago: University of Chicago Press, 1966).

24. See Richard M. Scammon and Ben J. Wattenberg, *The Real Majority* (New York: Coward-McCann, 1970), especially pp. 35–44.

25. Lanny J. Davis, *The Emerging Democratic Majority: Lessons and Legacies from the New Politics* (New York: Stein and Day, 1974), p. 61.

26. "Opponents See Duffey's Victory as a Benefit to Them in November," *New York Times,* 21 August 1970, p. 25.

27. "Bailey Sees Senatorial Primary in Connecticut on Wednesday as a Close Contest," *New York Times*, 16 August 1970, p. 29.

28. Davis, *Emerging Democratic Majority*, p. 62.

29. "Lawyer Becomes Fourth Candidate to Oppose Dodd," *New York Times*, 2 June 1970, p. 30.

30. This analysis excludes Donahue's hometown, Stamford. Primary percentages are derived from statistics furnished by the Office of the Secretary of State of Connecticut. Percentages on levels of education are from the Department of Commerce, *Nineteenth Decennial Census, 1970*.

31. Clark University, Public Affairs Research Center, combined Massachusetts surveys, October 1978, February and March 1979.

32. University of Connecticut, Institute for Social Inquiry, combined Connecticut polls, April, November, and December 1979, and February 1981. Similarly, in these surveys, 15 percent of non-college-educated and 47 percent of college-educated Connecticut Democrats opposed the death penalty for the killing of an on-duty police officer; 56 and 36 percent, respectively, favored preserving jobs over protecting the environment; and 58 and 38 percent, respectively, labeled homosexual relations as "basically wrong."

33. Clark University, Public Affairs Research Center, press release, 9 March 1978.

34. Survey conducted for Edward J. King by Baraff, Morris and Mercurio Associates, New York, March 1978.

35. "King Pins Hopes on New Poll," *Boston Globe*, 13 January 1978.

36. "King Hammered Away at Gut Level Issues," *Boston Herald American*, 21 September 1978.

37. Author's tape recording of Massachusetts gubernatorial candidates' debate, 31 August 1978.

38. "Senate Sustains Dukakis Death Penalty Veto," *New York Times*, 2 May 1975, p. 23.

39. King campaign advertisement, *Boston Globe*, 18 September 1978.

40. "The Campaign Quotes," *Boston Globe*, 5 November 1978.

41. Interview with Edward J. King, Boston, 7 January 1982.

42. Interview with Michael S. Dukakis, Cambridge, 6 January 1982.

43. Clark University, Public Affairs Research Center, Massachusetts survey, October 1978; Baraff, Morris and Mercurio, survey for King.

44. Clark University, Public Affairs Research Center, Massachusetts survey, October 1978.

45. "Dukakis Holds Back on King Endorsement," *Boston Globe*, 21 September 1978; p. 1; interview with Dukakis, Cambridge, 30 October 1979.

46. David B. Wilson, "He Means What He Says, Says What He Means," *Boston Globe*, 2 October 1978, p. 17.

47. Interview with Dukakis, 30 October 1979.

48. "O'Neill Will Run with King," *Boston Globe*, 22 September 1978, p. 1.

49. "Jarvis Takes to Bay State Television to Give King Candidacy a Boost," *Boston Globe*, 3 November 1978, p. 1.

50. Interview with Thomas P. "Tip" O'Neill, Jr., Washington, D.C., 22 September 1982.

51. Interview with Marcia Molay, Boston, 5 January 1982. In April 1982 the Massachusetts Supreme Judicial Court upheld a Democratic Party Charter provision that imposed a 15 percent rule on the party convention. The charter provision, previously nonbinding, became mandatory. The court's ruling took the form of an advisory opinion to Governor King (at his request) and was dated 23 April 1982.

52. Interview with Paul E. Tsongas, Washington, D.C., 15 August 1982.

53. Interview with Chester G. Atkins, Boston, 6 January 1982.

54. Interview with John N. Dempsey, Sr., Groton, Conn., 4 December 1979.

55. "Ribicoff Sorry He Quit as Governor," *Hartford Courant*, 11 May 1979, p. 21.

56. See note 51, above.

57. Interview with Dodd.

58. Department of Commerce, *Nineteenth Decennial Census*, 1970. The other states with a high percentage of the workforce in blue-collar occupations are South Carolina, North Carolina, West Virginia, Maine, Alabama, Indiana, Tennessee, New Hampshire, Pennsylvania, Kentucky, and Mississippi.

59. "Adamant McGarry Says No; Will Not Support McGovern," *Providence Journal*, 12 July 1972, p. 6.

60. "Rhode Island Democrats' Anti-Abortion Plank at Odds with National Party Platform," *Providence Journal*, 13 October 1976, p. B-1.

61. Interview with J. Joseph Garrahy, Providence, 6 November 1979.

62. Ibid.

63. The Rhode Island nomination system is one of the most liberal in the region. To force a primary, a candidate must obtain a specified number of signatures of registered voters, exactly as they appear on the voter registry: 1,000 to run in a gubernatorial or U.S. senatorial primary, 500 to qualify for a congressional or state office. A widely accepted rule is that a candidate should obtain twice the number of required signatures in order to be assured of having the necessary number of valid signatures.

64. Interview with Edward P. Beard, Washington, D.C., 19 October 1979.

65. Interview with Philip W. Noel, Providence, 24 October 1979.

66. Interview with John E. Murphy, Jr., Boston, 8 January 1982.

67. Interview with Dukakis, 30 October 1979.

68. CBS News/*New York Times*, "Massachusetts Primary Day Poll," press release, 4 March 1980.

69. In the state's Democratic presidential primary, South Boston's vote

was 50 percent for Carter, 45 percent for Kennedy and 5 percent for Brown. In the general election South Boston gave Reagan 50 percent of its votes; 42 percent went to Carter, 8 percent to Anderson.

Chapter 4

1. "Help Wanted: GOP in Massachusetts Advertises for Candidates," *Providence Journal*, 13 August 1978, p. B-2.

2. "Committee Urges GOP Deficit Group," *Hartford Courant*, 15 December 1978, p. 56.

3. "Raffle Bankrupts Stafford Republicans," *Hartford Courant*, 18 September 1980.

4. Interview with Jack Zaiman, Hartford, 16 July 1979.

5. "GOP Slide Continues Downward," *Hartford Courant*, 28 January 1979, p. 39.

6. "Stafford GOP Trying, but God Must Be a Democrat," *Hartford Courant*, 29 October 1978, p. 39.

7. Telephone interview with R. E. Van Norstrand, 20 January 1981.

8. "In Rhode Island It's Volatile Republican against Low-Key Democrat," *Boston Globe*, 16 October 1980, p. 34.

9. "GOP May Disappear—Buckley," *Boston Herald American*, 8 November 1978.

10. "The State GOP's Disintegration," *Boston Herald*, 23 September 1974, p. 11.

11. Interview with Barney Frank, Boston, 31 October 1979.

12. Interview with Gordon M. Nelson, Boston, 30 October 1979.

13. Robert L. Turner, "Tough Times for the State GOP," *Boston Globe*, 23 September 1980, p. 11.

14. Interview with Francis W. Sargent, Boston, 24 October 1979.

15. Interview with John E. Murphy, Jr., Boston, 8 January 1982.

16. "State GOP Fights Hard for a Brighter Future," *Boston Globe*, 2 September 1972, p. 5.

17. Telephone interview with Andrew S. Natsios, 1 March 1982.

18. "Young GOP Unit Urged to Keep Party United," *Providence Journal*, 14 June 1976. Chafee repeated the opinion in an interview in Washington, D.C., 19 October 1979.

19. "New England Voters Show Favor for Conservatives and New Faces," *New York Times*, 9 November 1978, p. A-24.

20. Massachusetts Republican Party, *State Platform* (Boston, 1978), p. 3.

21. In Rhode Island the GOP constitutes less than one-fifth of the House and Senate, far short of the two-fifths required to sustain a veto. In Massachusetts the Republicans are six seats short of the one-third needed to sustain a gubernatorial veto in the Senate, and twenty-two seats short in the House.

22. Massachusetts Secretary of the Commonwealth, *Massachusetts Election Statistics, 1960–1980* (Boston, 1980); *Manual for the General Assembly of Rhode Island, 1980.*

23. *Connecticut Register and Manual, 1979–1980.*

24. Interview with Donald Roch, Providence, 22 October 1979.

25. Interview with Murphy.

26. Interview with Patrick J. Halley, Boston, 29 October 1979.

27. Interview with John O. Pastore, Providence, 24 October 1979.

28. Interview with Frank.

29. "Why the Republicans Lost," interview with Republican State Chairman Frederick K. Biebel, *Hartford Courant,* 12 November 1978, p. 39.

30. Telephone interview with Natsios.

31. *Report of the Rhode Island Republican Party Image Committee: A Factual Analysis of the Present Party Image and Recommendations on How to Improve It* (Providence: Americo Campanella, Republican State Party Chairman, 1977), p. 7.

32. V. O. Key, Jr., *Southern Politics in State and Nation* (New York: Alfred A. Knopf, 1949), pp. 277, 292–93.

33. Interview with Nelson.

34. Ibid.

35. Interview with Vincent A. Cianci, Providence, 15 November 1979.

36. Interview with Roch.

37. "Brooke Is Safe But . . . ," *Boston Globe,* 31 October 1971, p. A-5.

38. Telephone interview with George Gunther, 25 January 1981.

39. *Report of the Rhode Island Republican Party Image Committee,* p. 5.

40. Interview with Ella T. Grasso, Hartford, 16 October 1979.

41. Interview with John Volpe, Nahant, Mass., 6 December 1979.

42. *Report of the Rhode Island Republican Party Image Committee,* p. 6.

43. Interview with Rocco Quattrocchi, Providence, 23 October 1979.

44. Interview with Frederick K. Biebel, Hartford, 17 October 1979.

45. *Report of the Rhode Island Republican Party Image Committee,* p. 7.

46. Interview with Quattrocchi. Quattrocchi runs his own heating oil firm.

47. Interview with John H. Chafee, Washington, D.C., 19 October 1979.

48. Ian S. Haberman, "The Rhode Island Business Elite, 1895–1905: A Collective Portrait," *Rhode Island History* 26 (April 1967): 38–39.

49. Interview with Warren A. Johnson, Boston, 28 December 1981.

50. Interview with Cianci.

51. Interview with Johnson, 28 December 1981.

52. Interview with Arthur J. Lumsden, Hartford, 16 October 1979.

53. Telephone interview with Anthony (Toby) Moffett, Washington, D.C., 2 January 1980.

54. Interview with Warren A. Johnson, Boston, 1 November 1979.

55. First National Bank of Boston, *New England Report,* Fall 1979, p. 4. The results for ideology 1 for other areas of the country were: Middle Atlan-

tic, 60 percent; Midwest, 64 percent; Southeast, 62 percent; South Central, 72 percent; Mountain, 70 percent; and Far West, 62 percent. For ideology 2 the results were 38 percent, 34 percent, 35 percent, 27 percent, 28 percent, and 36 percent, respectively.

56. Interview with Johnson, 1 November 1979.

57. Interview with Sargent.

58. Quoted in Edward W. Brooke, *The Challenge of Change: Crisis in Our Two-Party System* (Boston: Little, Brown, 1966), p. 91.

59. Ibid.

60. Ibid., p. 92.

61. Quoted in Everett Carll Ladd, *Where Have All the Voters Gone?* (New York: W. W. Norton, 1978), p. 19.

62. Interview with Michael S. Dukakis, Cambridge, 30 October 1979.

63. "Senator Atkins on Massachusetts GOP: Obsessed with Ideology," *Boston Globe*, 13 November 1979, p. 8.

64. Edgar Litt, *The Political Cultures of Massachusetts* (Cambridge, Mass.: MIT Press, 1965), p. 24.

65. Interview with John A. Holmes, Jr., Providence, 8 July 1981.

66. Interview with R. E. Van Norstrand, Hartford, 17 October 1979.

67. Lowell Weicker, address to Republican State Convention, Hartford, 28 July 1978.

68. Interview with Biebel.

69. In an interview in Hartford 18 June 1981, Republican State Chairman Capecelatro said, "Senator Weicker has told me, 'That budget may fly in Nevada or California, but it won't fly in Connecticut.'"

70. ADA ratings for 1980 were as follows: southern New England Democrats, 73 percent, and southern New England Republicans, 74 percent; Democrats nationwide, 58 percent; and Republicans nationwide, 15 percent; *Congressional Quarterly Weekly*, (1981).

71. "Bay State ADA Finds GOP 'Real Liberals,'" *Boston Globe*, 3 April 1969, p. 1.

72. John H. Kessel, *The Goldwater Coalition: Republican Strategies in 1964* (New York: Bobbs-Merrill, 1968), p. 238.

73. In 1964 Goldwater received only 19 percent of the votes of the southern New England Republican convention delegates. In 1968, 94 percent of the region's delegates sided with Nelson Rockefeller against the eventual GOP nominee, Richard Nixon. Nixon's renomination was unanimous in 1972. Southern New England delegates overwhelmingly preferred Ford over Reagan in 1976, 84 percent to 16 percent. In 1980 the tristate area sided overwhelmingly with Reagan although nine delegates from Massachusetts voted for John Anderson.

74. Interview with Holmes.

75. Massachusetts Republican Party, *State Platform 1974* (Boston, 1974), p. 1.

76. Fenton Futtner, to the author, 7 February 1979.

77. Nelson W. Polsby and Aaron B. Wildavsky, *Presidential Elections* (New York: Charles Scribner's Sons, 1971), pp. 38–39.

78. "Weicker Wants Eligibility Test," *Hartford Courant*, 19 April 1979, p. 8.

79. Telephone interview with Van Norstrand, 20 January 1981.

80. Interview with Van Norstrand, 17 October 1979.

81. Ibid.

82. Interview with Frederick Lippitt, Providence, 26 October 1979.

83. Interview with Holmes.

84. "'New Right' Group Has a Little Old and a Lot New," *Boston Herald Traveler*, 26 March 1972, p. 20.

85. Interview with Nelson.

86. Ibid.

87. Francis W. Hatch, "A Candidate's Afterthoughts: Frank Hatch Relives His Campaign," *Boston Globe*, 25 February 1979, p. B-1.

88. Interview with Nelson.

89. Hatch, "A Candidate's Afterthoughts," p. B-1.

90. "Senator Atkins on Massachusetts GOP." Sargent later repeated the charge in an interview, 24 October 1979.

91. Interview with Sargent.

92. Ibid.

93. Interview with Iris K. Holland, Boston, 1 November 1979.

94. Interview with Ronald Civins-Mills, Providence, 23 October 1979.

95. Interview with Thomas P. "Tip" O'Neill, Jr., Washington, D.C., 22 September 1982.

96. "The State of the GOP in Massachusetts," *Boston Globe*, 12 November 1978, p. 38.

97. In 1900 Democrats constituted 8 and 21 percent of the Connecticut Senate and House of Representatives, respectively. Today the Republicans are in better shape (particularly after the 1980 elections), holding 36 and 45 percent of the seats in the state Senate and House of Representatives. In Massachusetts and Rhode Island the 1900 Democratic percentage of seats is comparable to today's GOP figures. In Massachusetts the Democrats held 15 and 25 percent of the seats in the state Senate and House in 1900; in 1981 the GOP percentages were 17 and 19 percent, respectively. Rhode Island Democrats held 8 and 17 percent of the seats in their Senate and House in 1900. Republicans in the 1981–1982 session of the General Assembly controlled 14 percent of Senate seats and 18 percent of the House membership. *Connecticut Register and Manual*, 1901 and 1981; *Manual for the General Court*, 1901 and 1979–1981; and *Manual for the General Assembly of Rhode Island*, 1901–1902 and 1981–1982.

Chapter 5

1. Recounted by James M. Howell in an interview, Boston, 16 January 1980.

2. Interview with Ray Stata, Norwood, Mass., 6 December 1979.

3. Interview with John N. Dempsey, Sr., Groton, Conn., 4 December 1979.

4. Interview with Erskine N. White, Providence, 23 October 1979.

5. Interview with Warren A. Johnson, Boston, 28 December 1981.

6. John S. Hekman, "What Attracts Industry to New England?" *New England Economic Indicators*, December 1978, p. A5.

7. Quoted in Kevin P. Phillips, *Mediacracy: American Parties and Politics in the Communications Age* (Garden City, N.Y.: Doubleday, 1975), p. 213.

8. "Battleground: Jobs Growth and Money Hinge on New War between the States," *Boston Globe*, 27 January 1980, p. 61.

9. ABC News / Louis Harris and Associates, press release, 3 March 1980.

10. Everett C. Ladd and G. Donald Ferree, Jr., "The Voting System, the Policy System, and the Current Malaise of Representative Government in the United States" (Paper presented at the annual meeting of the American Political Science Association, Washington, D.C., 22 September 1979), pp. 23a, 23h.

11. Interview with William A. O'Neill, Hartford, 15 October 1979.

12. Interview with Jack Zaiman, Hartford, 16 July 1979.

13. Interview with Michael S. Dukakis, Cambridge, 30 October 1979.

14. Maurice Duverger, *Political Parties: Their Organization and Activity in the Modern State* (London: Lowe and Brydone, 1964), p. 61.

15. Clinton Rossiter, *Parties and Politics in America* (Ithaca, N.Y.: Cornell University Press, 1960).

16. Interview with R. E. Van Norstrand, Hartford, 17 October 1979.

17. E. E. Schattschneider, *The Semisovereign People: A Realist's View of Democracy in America* (Hinsdale, Ill.: Dryden Press, 1975), p. 69.

18. Interview with Chester G. Atkins, Boston, 29 October 1979.

19. Interview with Christopher J. Dodd, Washington, D.C., 19 October 1979.

20. Interview with James M. Fitzgerald, Hartford, 19 June 1981.

21. Telephone interview with Andrew S. Natsios, 16 September 1980.

22. Interview with Thomas P. O'Neill III, Boston, 15 July 1982.

23. Telephone interview with Andrew S. Natsios, 1 March 1982.

24. Quoted in Sanford F. Schram, "Accommodationist Political Parties as Agents of Democratic Elitism: Democratic Theory in the Critique of Party Reform" (Research paper, 1982).

25. "The Campaign Quotes," *Boston Globe*, 5 November 1978, p. A-5. The statement was allegedly made by Angelo Berlandi, a King aide, shortly after the Democratic primary. King states that Berlandi denies making the comment.

26. Interview with James M. Howell, Boston, 8 January 1982.

27. Interview with Edward Reilly, Boston, 5 January 1982.

28. Interview with Michael S. Dukakis, Cambridge, 6 January 1982.

29. Ibid.

30. Interview with Reilly.

31. Interview with John E. Murphy, Jr., Boston, 8 January 1982.

32. ABC News/Louis Harris and Associates, press releases, 14 March 1977, 5 January 1978, 25 September 1978, and 5 March 1979.

33. University of Chicago, National Opinion Research Center, general social surveys, 1972–1978, cumulative.

34. Robert L. Turner, "GOP's Lakian Banks on Alienated Voter," *Boston Globe*, 14 March 1982, p. A-25. The question: "Instead of being the servants of the people, elected officials in Massachusetts are really the enemy of the people." The results: 14 percent "strongly agree," 26 percent "somewhat agree," 32 percent "somewhat disagree," 20 percent "strongly disagree," 8 percent "no opinion, don't know."

35. Those expressing "a great deal of confidence" in the military declined from 62 percent in 1966 to 27 percent in 1971, increasing slightly to 29 percent in 1979; for Congress, the proportion was 42 percent in 1966, 19 percent in 1971, and 18 percent in 1979; for the executive branch, 41 percent in 1966, 23 percent in 1971, and 17 percent in 1979.

36. ABC News/Harris press releases, 14 March 1977, 5 January 1978, 25 September 1978, and 5 March 1979.

37. Interview with Howell, 8 January 1982.

38. Interview with Thomas P. O'Neill, Jr., Washington, D.C., 22 September 1982.

Postscript

1. "Heckler, Frank Clash Again in Fourth and Final Debate," *Boston Globe*, 12 October 1982, p. 23.

2. "The Reagan Issue in Rhode Island Race," *Boston Globe*, 23 September 1982, p. 17.

3. "Sixth District Contest Is Bruising Battle," *Hartford Courant*, 28 October 1982, p. C-1.

4. "The Role of Reaganomics in Massachusetts Politics," *Boston Globe*, 31 October 1982, p. 18.

5. "The Mixed Bag of N.E. Returns," *Boston Globe*, 4 November 1982, p. 29.

6. Samuel Lubell, *The Future of American Politics* (New York: Harper & Row, 1965), p. 13.

7. Edward M. Kennedy to the author, 24 January 1983.

8. "Locke Gets 7–10 Years," *Boston Globe*, 18 February 1982, p. 1.

9. "King, Dukakis and the Polls," *Boston Globe*, 19 September 1982, p. 1.

10. "War of the Media Wizards," *Boston Globe*, 19 September 1982, p. A-1.

11. Interview with Peter Y. Flynn, Boston, 14 July 1982.

12. Survey of Massachusetts Democratic convention delegates, 22 May 1982. Of 3,481 delegates, 646 responses were received. The author wishes to acknowledge the assistance of Professor Jerome M. Mileur of the University of Massachusetts in conducting the survey.

13. Ibid.

14. These are unofficial primary results. See "Democrat for Governor / The City and Town Primary Vote," *Boston Globe*, 16 September 1982, p. 30. After the primary election, King endorsed the Democratic ticket. However, he refused to campaign actively for Dukakis citing the latter's position on abortion.

15. Survey of Massachusetts Democratic Convention Delegates, 22 May 1982.

16. Ibid.

17. "Of Spats and Keeping Score," *Boston Globe*, 23 May 1982, p. 84. Kennedy, however, lost South Boston, the family's ancestral home, to Republican Ray Shamie.

18. "Democrat Runs Quietly in Massachusetts Race," *New York Times*, 25 October 1982, p. B-6.

19. "Republicans Look Out from Down Under," *Boston Globe*, 4 November 1982, p. 25.

20. Ibid.

21. "Kennedy, An Easy Winner, Keeps Presidential Hopes," *Providence Journal*, 3 November 1982, p. A-14.

22. "Facing Reality: All Uphill for GOP," *Boston Globe*, 6 June 1982, p. A-33.

23. "Republicans Look Out from Down Under," p. 25.

24. These are unofficial results. See "Schneider with 56% Turns Back Aukerman," *Providence Journal*, 3 November 1982, p. A-18.

25. "'Mr. Republican' Seeks Party Anonymity," *Hartford Courant*, 24 October 1982, p. A-9.

26. "Marzullo Wants Two-Party System," *Providence Journal*, 26 October 1982, p. A-8.

27. "They Didn't Need the Yellow Pages to Find Garrahy," *Providence Journal*, 13 June 1982, p. I-14.

;28. "Garrahy Has Problems but His Opposition Is Weak," *Providence Journal*, 17 October 1982, p. B-1.

29. These are unofficial election returns. See "Election Results," *Providence Journal*, 3 November 1982, p. A-1.

30. Because of a redistricting squabble, elections to the Rhode Island state Senate were postponed until January 1983.

31. "Mayor Walsh Wins Again, Gets 87% of the Vote, Promises More Good Government," *Providence Journal*, 3 November 1982, p. C-1.

32. "GOP Goes 'Back to Basics' to Rebuild and Win Elections," *Providence Journal*, 20 September 1982, p. C-4.

33. "Winners and Losers Start Looking to the Future," *Providence Journal*, 7 November 1982, p. B-1.

34. "Democrats Widen Registration Gap," *Hartford Courant*, 27 October 1982, p. C-3.

35. "Bush's Brother, Connecticut Party Leaders Drive to Unseat GOP's Bad Boy," *Providence Journal*, 18 July 1982, p. B-1.

36. "Weicker Assails Two Rivals in Connecticut Senate-Race Debate, *New York Times*, 28 October 1970, p. 34.

37. "Agnew Calls Lindsay a 'Conglomerate,'" *New York Times*, 24 October 1970, p. 12.

38. "Memo to William O'Neill . . . and Lowell Weicker," *Hartford Courant* (ed.), 3 November 1982, p. A-22.

39. "Stands Fog Weicker's Identity," *Hartford Courant*, 13 June 1982, p. 1.

40. Tape recording of Weicker's 1982 GOP Convention Address. In the speech Weicker argued that the school prayer and busing amendments would transform the U.S. Constitution "into a trash basket for transient political issues."

41. Ibid.

42. Unofficial election results. See "Weicker Over Moffett," *Hartford Courant*, 3 November 1982, p. A-1.

43. Ibid.

44. Ibid.

45. Ibid.

46. Interview with Ralph A. Capecelatro, Hartford, 18 June 1981.

BIBLIOGRAPHY

Printed Matter

Alvarez, David J. and Edmund J. True. "Critical Elections and Partisan Re-alignment: An Urban Test Case." *Polity* 5, no. 4 (Summer 1973): 573–76.

Barbrook, Alex. *God Save the Commonwealth: An Electoral History of Massachusetts*. Amherst: University of Massachusetts Press, 1973.

Bell, Daniel. *The Coming of Post-Industrial Society*. New York: Basic Books, 1973.

Boston, City of. *Documents of the City of Boston, 1977*. Boston, 1977.

Brewer, Daniel Chauncey. *The Conquest of New England by the Immigrant*. New York: G. P. Putnam and Sons, 1926.

Briggs, B. Bruce, ed. *The New Class?* New Brunswick, N.J.: Transaction Books, 1979.

Broder, David S. *The Party's Over: The Failure of Politics in America*. New York: Harper & Row, 1972.

Brooke, Edward W. *The Challenge of Change: Crisis in Our Two-Party System*. Boston: Little, Brown, 1966.

Brzezinski, Zbigniew. *Between Two Ages: America's Role in the Technetronic Era*. New York: Viking Press, 1970.

Burck, Charles G. "A Group Portrait of the Fortune 500 Chief Executive." *Fortune* (May 1976): 173–77, 308–12.

Burner, David. *The Politics of Provincialism: The Democratic Party in Transition, 1918–1932*. New York: Alfred A. Knopf, 1968.

Burtt, Everett J., Jr. *Influence of Labor Supply on Location of Electronics Firms*. Research Report No. 34. Boston: Federal Reserve Bank of Boston, 1966.

Campbell, Angus; Philip E. Converse; Warren Miller; and Donald Stokes. *The American Voter*. New York: John Wiley and Sons, 1964.

Carroll, Leo E. "Irish and Italians in Providence, Rhode Island, 1880–1970." *Rhode Island History* (Summer 1969): 67–74.

Clubb, Jerome M., and Howard W. Allen. "The Cities and the Election of 1928: Partisan Realignment?" *American Historical Review* 74 (April 1969): 1205–20.

Connecticut Democratic Party. *State Platform, 1920; State Platform, 1924; State Platform, 1928.* Hartford, 1920, 1924, 1928.

Connecticut Department of Commerce. *1978 Market Data: Connecticut.* Hartford, 1978.

Connecticut Development Commission, Research and Information Division. *Community Monographs: East Hartford, Connecticut, 1970.* Hartford, 1970.

Connecticut Republican Party. *State Platform, 1892; State Platform, 1934; State Platform, 1936.* Hartford, 1892, 1934, 1936.

Connecticut, State of. *State of Connecticut Register and Manual, 1900 through 1981.* Hartford, 1900–1981.

Coopers & Lybrand. *Result of Survey on Human Resource Needs.* Boston: Massachusetts High Technology Council, 1980.

Curley, James Michael. *I'd Do It Again: A Record of All My Uproarious Years.* Englewood Cliffs, New Jersey: Prentice-Hall, 1957.

Davis, Lanny J. *The Emerging Democratic Majority: Lessons and Legacies From the New Politics.* New York: Stein and Day, 1974.

de Tocqueville, Alexis. *Democracy in America.* Reprint. New York: New American Library, 1956. Originally published in 1835.

Deutermann, Elizabeth P. "Seeding Science-Based Industry." *New England Business Review* (December 1966).

Duverger, Maurice. *Political Parties: Their Organization and Activity in the Modern State.* London: Lowe and Brydone, 1964.

East Hartford Chamber of Commerce. *East Hartford . . . Paved for Progress* East Hartford, Conn., 1957.

Estle, Edwin F. "The Region's Roving Industries." *New England Business Review* (June 1967).

First National Bank of Boston. *New England Report,* Fall 1979.

Gabriel, Richard A. *Ethnic Voting in Primary Elections: The Case of Providence, Rhode Island.* Kingston: University of Rhode Island, Bureau of Government Research, 1969.

———. *The Political Machine in Rhode Island.* Kingston: University of Rhode Island, Bureau of Government Research, 1970.

Glantz, Frederick B. *The Geographic Mobility of Labor in New England.* Boston: Federal Reserve Bank of Boston, 1975.

Glazer, Nathan and Daniel Patrick Moynihan. *Beyond the Melting Pot: The Negroes, Puerto Ricans, Jews, Italians and Irish of New York City.* Cambridge, Mass.: MIT Press, 1970.

Goodman, Jay S. *The Democrats and Labor in Rhode Island, 1952–1962: Changes in the Old Alliance.* Providence: Brown University Press, 1967.

Goodwin, George, Jr., and Robert B. Dishman. *State Legislatures in New England Politics: Final Report of the New England Assembly on State*

Legislatures, September 10–13, 1967. Durham, N.H.: New England Center for Continuing Education, 1967.

Greenstein, David M. "The Rhode Island Democratic Party: From Unity to Disunity." Master's thesis, University of Rhode Island, 1966.

Haberman, Ian S. "The Rhode Island Business Elite, 1895–1905: A Collective Portrait." *Rhode Island History* 26 (April 1967): 38–39.

Handlin, Oscar. *Al Smith and His America*. Boston: Little, Brown, 1958.

————. *Boston Immigrants: A Study in Acculturation*. Cambridge, Mass.: Harvard University Press, 1959.

————. *Immigration as a Factor in American History*. Englewood Cliffs, N.J.: Prentice-Hall, 1959.

Hartford, City of. *Court of Common Council: Municipal Register, 1920*. Hartford: Bond Press, 1920.

Hartz, Louis. *The Liberal Tradition in America: An Interpretation of American Political Thought since the Revolution*. New York: Harcourt Brace Jovanovich, 1955.

Hekman, John S., "What Attracts Industry to New England?" *New England Economic Indicators*, December 1978.

Hekman, John S. and John S. Strong. "The Evolution of New England Industry," *New England Economic Review*, March/April 1981.

Hess, Stephen, and David S. Broder. *The Republican Establishment: The Present and Future of the G.O.P.* New York: Harper & Row, 1967.

Huthmacher, J. Joseph. *Massachusetts: People and Politics, 1919–1933*. New York: Atheneum, 1969.

————. *A Nation of Newcomers: Ethnic Minorities in American History*. New York: Delacorte Press, 1967.

Jackson, Francis. *History of the Early Settlement of Newton, County of Middlesex, Massachusetts*. Boston: Stacy and Richardson, 1854.

Kessel, John H. *The Goldwater Coalition: Republican Strategies in 1964*. New York: Bobbs-Merrill, 1968.

Key, V. O., Jr. *American State Politics: An Introduction*. New York: Alfred A. Knopf, 1965.

————. *Politics, Parties, and Pressure Groups*. 5th ed. New York: Thomas Y. Crowell, 1964.

————. *Southern Politics in State and Nation*. New York: Alfred A. Knopf, 1949.

————. "A Theory of Critical Elections." *Journal of Politics* 17 (February 1955): 3–18.

Koenig, Samuel. *Immigrant Settlements in Connecticut: Their Growth and Characteristics*. Hartford: Connecticut State Department of Education, 1938.

Ladd, Everett Carll. *American Political Parties: Social Change and Political Response*. New York: W. W. Norton, 1970.

————. *Ideology in America: Change and Response in a City, a Suburb, and a Small Town*. New York: W. W. Norton, 1972.

————. "The New Divisions in U.S. Politics." *Fortune*, 26 March 1979, pp. 88–96.

————. "What the Voters Really Want." *Fortune*, 18 December 1978, pp. 40–48.

————. *Where Have All the Voters Gone?* New York: W. W. Norton, 1978.

————. Ladd, Everett Carll, and G. Donald Ferree, Jr. "The Voting System, the Policy System, and the Current Malaise of Representative Government in the United States." Paper presented at the annual meeting of the American Political Science Association, Washington, D.C., 22 September 1979.

Ladd, Everett Carll, and Seymour Martin Lipset. *The Divided Academy: Professors and Politics*. New York: McGraw-Hill, 1975.

Ladd, Everett Carll, and G. Donald Ferree, Jr. "The Voting System, the Policy System, and the Current Malaise of Representative Government in the United States." Paper presented at the annual meeting of the American Political Science Association, Washington, D.C., 22 September 1979.

Lakis, Stephen G., ed. *The Almanac: Massachusetts State Officials, 1981–1982*. Boston: Almanac Research Services, 1981.

Latham, Earl. *Massachusetts Politics*. New York: Citizenship Clearing House, 1957.

Levin, Murray B., with George Blackwood. *The Compleat Politician: Political Strategy in Massachusetts*. New York: Bobbs-Merrill, 1962.

Levy, Mark R., and Michael S. Cramer. *The Ethnic Factor: How America's Minorities Decide Elections*. New York: Simon and Schuster, 1972.

Lieberman, Joseph I. *The Power Broker: A Biography of John M. Bailey, Modern Political Boss*. Boston: Houghton Mifflin, 1966.

Litt, Edgar. *Ethnic Politics in America*. Glenview, Ill.: Scott, Foresman, 1970.

————. *The Political Cultures of Massachusetts*. Cambridge, Mass.: MIT Press, 1965.

Lockard, Duane. *New England State Politics*. Princeton: Princeton University Press, 1959.

Lowell, James Russell. "New England Two Centuries Ago." In *Literary Essays*, Vol. 2. Boston: Houghton Mifflin, 1890.

Lubell, Samuel. *The Future of American Politics*. 3d ed. New York: Harper & Row, 1965.

Massachusetts Democratic Party. *Charter Provisions, State Platform of the Democratic Party of the Commonwealth of Massachusetts: 1981*. Boston, 1981.

————. *State Platform, 1910; State Platform, 1913; State Platform, 1978*. Boston, 1910, 1913, 1978.

Massachusetts. Department of Commerce and Development. *Comprehensive Cost Profile High-Technology Electronics Manufacturing*. Boston, 1978.

————. *Profile of Newton*. Boston, 1976.

Massachusetts General Court. *A Manual for the Use of the General Court, 1900 through 1981–1982*. Boston, 1901–1982.

Massachusetts Occupation Industry Research Department, Research and Information Service. *Employment Requirements for Massachusetts by Occupation, by Industry, 1970–1974–1985*. Boston, 1976.

Massachusetts Republican Party. *State Platform, 1913; State Platform, 1928; State Platform, 1974*. Boston, 1913, 1928, 1974.

Massachusetts Secretary of the Commonwealth. *Massachusetts Election Statistics, 1960–1980*. Public Document No. 43. Boston, 1981.

Massachusetts State Industrial Directory, 1977. New York: State Industrial Directories Corporation, 1977.

Mayhew, David R. *Two-Party Competition in the New England States*. Amherst: University of Massachusetts, Bureau of Government Research, 1967.

McCarthy, James E. *Trade Adjustment Assistance: A Case Study of the Shoe Industry in Massachusetts*. Research Report No. 58. Boston: Federal Reserve Bank of Boston, 1975.

Milburn, Josephine F., and Victoria Schuck. *New England Politics*. Cambridge, Mass.: Schenkman, 1981.

Mileur, Jerome M., and George T. Sulzner. *Campaigning for the Massachusetts Senate: Electioneering Outside the Political Limelight*. Amherst: University of Massachusetts Press, 1974.

Moos, Malcolm. *The Republicans: A History of Their Party*. New York; Random House, 1956.

"New England: Fighting to Make a Comeback." *U.S. News & World Report*, 1 January 1973.

"New England: What Replaces Old Industry?" *Business Week*, 4 August 1979, pp. 36–41.

Ogburn, William, and Nell Talbot. "A Measurement of the Factors in the Presidential Election of 1928." *Social Forces* 8 (December 1929): pp. 175–83.

Paquette, Lee. *Only More So: The History of East Hartford, 1783–1976*. East Hartford, Conn.: Raymond Library, 1976.

Peirce, Neal R. *The New England States: People, Politics, and Power in the Six New England States*. New York: W. W. Norton, 1976.

Phillips, Kevin P. *The Emerging Republican Majority*. New Rochelle, N.Y.: Arlington House, 1969.

————. *Mediacracy: American Parties and Politics in the Communications Age*. Garden City, N.Y.: Doubleday, 1975.

Polsby, Nelson W., and Aaron B. Wildavsky. *Presidential Elections*. New York: Charles Scribner's Sons, 1971.

Project Rhode Island. *The Rhode Island Economy: A Plan for the Future*. Providence, 1972.

Ranney, Austin. "Parties in State Politics." In *Politics in the American*

States. Edited by Herbert Jacob and Kenneth Vines. Boston: Little, Brown, 1971.

Reiter, Howard L. "Carter's Catholic Problem, or Why Ford Carried Connecticut (and Other Bailiwicks)." Paper presented at the annual meeting of the Northeastern Political Science Association, Mount Pocono, Pa., 11 November 1977.

Rhode Island Department of Economic Development. *Central Falls: Rhode Island City and Town Monographs*. Providence, 1976.

―――. *Plant Financing and Financial Resources*. Providence, 1976.

―――. *Rhode Island: Basic Statistics, 1977–1978*. Providence, 1979.

―――. *Rhode Island: Basic Statistics, 1979–1980*. Providence, 1981.

Rhode Island General Assembly. *Manual with Rules and Orders for the Use of the General Assembly of the State of Rhode Island, 1901–02 through 1981–1982*. Providence, 1902–1982.

Rhode Island Historical Preservation Commission. *Central Falls, Rhode Island: Statewide Historical Preservation Report*. Providence, 1978.

Rhode Island Republican Party Image Committee. *Report of the Rhode Island Republican Party Image Committee: A Factual Analysis of the Present Party Image and Recommendations on How to Improve It*. Providence, 1977.

Rhode Island, State of. *Census*. Providence, 1865.

Ribicoff, Abraham, and Jon O. Newman. *Politics: The American Way*. Boston: Allyn and Bacon, 1967.

Richta, Radovan. *Civilization at the Crosroads: Social and Human Implications of the Scientific and Technological Revolution*. Prague, Czechoslovakia: International Arts and Sciences Press, 1969.

Rossiter, Clinton. *Parties and Politics in America*. Ithaca, N.Y.: Cornell University Press, 1960.

Scammon, Richard M. *America at the Polls: The Vote for President, 1920–1964*. Pittsburgh: University of Pittsburgh Press, 1965.

―――. *America Votes, 1960; America Votes, 1962*. Pittsburgh: University of Pittsburgh Press, 1962, 1964.

―――. *America Votes, 1964; America Votes, 1966; America Votes, 1968; America Votes, 1970; America Votes, 1972; America Votes, 1974*. Washington, D.C.: Congressional Quarterly, 1966, 1968, 1970, 1972, 1973, 1975.

Scammon, Richard M., and Alice V. McGillivray. *America Votes, 1976; America Votes, 1978*. Washington, D.C.: Congressional Quarterly, 1977, 1979.

Scammon, Richard M., and Ben J. Wattenberg. *The Real Majority*. New York: Coward-McCann, 1970.

Schattschneider, E.E. *The Semisovereign People: A Realist's View of Democracy in America*. Hinsdale, Ill.: Dryden Press, 1975.

Silva, Ruth. *Rum, Religion, and Votes: 1928 Re-examined*. University Park, Pa.: State University Press, 1962.

Smith, Alfred E. *Up to Now: An Autobiography*. New York: Viking Press, 1929.

Smith, S. F. *History of Newton, Massachusetts*. Boston: American Logotype Company, 1880.

Swanson, Wayne Richard. "An Analysis of Political Competition in Three New England States: Vermont, Massachusetts, and Rhode Island." Master's thesis, University of Rhode Island, 1965.

U.S. Census Office. *Twelfth Census of the United States Taken in the Year 1900*. Washington, D.C., 1901.

U.S. Department of Commerce and Labor, Bureau of the Census. *Thirteenth Census of the United States Taken in the Year 1910; Fourteenth Census of the United States Taken in the Year 1920; Fifteenth Census of the United States: 1930; The Sixteenth Census of the United States: 1940*. Washington, D.C., 1943; *The Seventeenth Census of the United States. Census of the Population: 1950*. Washington, D.C., 1953; *The Eighteenth Decennial Census of the United States. Census of the Population: 1960*. Washington, D.C., 1961; *The Nineteenth Decennial Census of the United States. Census of the Population: 1970*. Washington, D.C., 1973.

———. *Historical Statistics of the United States: Colonial Times to 1970*. Washington, D.C., 1975.

———. *Statistical Abstract of the United States, 1979*. Washington, D.C., 1979.

U.S. Department of the Interior, Bureau of the Census. *The Seventh Census of the United States: 1850*. Washington, D.C., 1853; *The Population of the United States in 1860*. Washington, D.C., 1864; *The Ninth Decennial Census of the United States: 1870*. Washington, D.C., 1872; *The Tenth Decennial Census of the United States: 1880*. Washington, D.C., 1883; *Report on Population of the United States at the Eleventh Census: 1890*. Washington, D.C., 1895.

———. *Statistics of Manufacturers, 1890: City of Newton, Massachusetts*. Census Bulletin No. 342. Washington, D.C., 1893.

U.S. Department of Labor, Bureau of Labor Statistics. *The Changing Structure of New England Employment, 1947–1973*. Washington, D.C., 1973.

Viorst, Milton. *Fall from Grace: The Republican Party and the Puritan Ethic*. New York: Simon and Schuster, 1971.

Warren, David D. "Hyphenated Americanism in Rhode Island Politics." *Alumni Bulletin of the University of Rhode Island* 3 (October 1964): 1–4.

Weicker, Lowell. Address to Republican State Convention, Hartford, 28 July 1978.

———. Address at the Glass Show, Hartford, 23 September 1978.

White, John K. "All in the Family: The 1978 Massachusetts Democratic Gubernatorial Primary." *Polity*, 14, no. 4 (Summer 1982): 641–56.

White, Theodore H. *The Making of the President, 1960; The Making of the President, 1964; The Making of the President, 1968; The Making of the President, 1972*. New York: Atheneum, 1961, 1965, 1969, 1973.

Wilson, James Q. *The Amateur Democrat: Club Politics in Three Cities*. Chicago: University of Chicago Press, 1966.

Witcover, Jules. *Marathon: The Pursuit of the Presidency, 1972–1976*. New York: Viking Press, 1977.

Woodrow Wilson International Center for Scholars. *Prospects for New England: Highlights of Proceedings and Supplementary Papers from a Conference at the Woodrow Wilson International Center for Scholars, October 7, 1974*. Washington, D.C., 1974.

Interviews

Atkins, Chester G. Boston. 29 October 1979 and 6 January 1982.

Beard, Edward P. Washington, D.C. 19 October 1979.

Biebel, Frederick K. Hartford. 17 October 1979.

Bozzuto, Richard C. Hartford. 17 October 1979.

Campanella, Americo. Providence. 25 October 1979.

Capecelatro, Ralph E. Hartford. 18 June 1981.

Chafee, John H. Washington, D.C. 19 October 1979.

Cianci, Vincent A. Providence. 15 November 1979.

Civins-Mills, Ronald. Providence. 23 October 1979.

Dempsey, John N., Jr. Hartford. 15 October 1979.

Dempsey, John N., Sr. Groton, Conn. 4 December 1979.

Dodd, Christopher J. Washington, D.C. 19 October 1979.

Dukakis, Michael S. Cambridge. 30 October 1979 and 6 January 1982.

Fitzgerald, James M. Hartford. 19 June 1981.

Flynn, Peter Y. Boston. 14 July 1982.

Frank, Barney. Boston. 31 October 1979.

Garrahy, J. Joseph. Providence. 6 November 1979.

Grasso, Ella T. Hartford. 16 October 1979.

Gunther, George. Telephone interview. 25 January 1981.

Halley, Patrick J. Boston. 29 October 1979.

Hatch, Francis W. Boston. 30 October 1979.

Holland, Iris K. Boston. 1 November 1979.

Holmes, John A., Jr. Providence. 8 July 1981.

Howell, James M. Boston. 16 January 1980 and 8 January 1982.

Hudak, Eva T. Torrington, Conn. 23 February 1980.

Johnson, Warren A. Boston. 1 November 1979 and 28 December 1981.

Kennedy, Edward M. Letter to the author. 24 January 1983.

King, Edward J. Boston. 7 January 1982.

Lawless, Joseph. Boston. 6 January 1982.

Licht, Frank. Providence. 25 October 1979.

Lieberman, Joseph I. Hartford. 22 January 1980.

Lippitt, Frederick. Providence. 26 October 1979.

Lumsden, Arthur J. Hartford. 16 October 1979.

MacDonald, Georgina. Providence. 3 August 1982.

Moffett, Anthony. 2 January 1980 (telephone).

Molay, Marcia. Boston. 5 January 1982.

Murphy, John E., Jr. Boston. 8 January 1982.

Natsios, Andrew S. 16 September 1980 (telephone) and 1 March 1982 (telephone).

Nelson, Gordon M. Boston. 30 October 1979.

Noel, Philip W. Providence. 24 October 1979.

O'Neill, Thomas P. "Tip", Jr. Washington, D.C. 22 September 1982.

O'Neill, Thomas P., III. Boston. 15 July 1982.

O'Neill, William A. Hartford. 15 October 1979.

Pastore, John O. Providence. 24 October 1979.

Pell, Claiborne. Washington, D.C. 19 October 1979.

Quattrocchi, Rocco. Providence. 23 October 1979.

Reilly, Edward. Boston. 5 January 1982.

Roch, Donald. Providence. 22 October 1979.

Sargent, Francis W. Boston. 24 October 1979.

Stata, Ray. Norwood, Mass. 6 December 1979.

Sullivan, David E. Boston. 5 January 1982.

Tsongas, Paul E. Washington, D.C. 15 August 1982.

Van Norstrand, Ralph E. Hartford. 17 October 1979 and 20 January 1981 (telephone).

Volpe, John A. Nahant, Mass. 6 December 1979.

Walsh, Joseph W. Warwick, R.I. 25 October 1979.

White, Erskine N. Providence. 23 October 1979.

Zaiman, Jack. Hartford. 16 July 1979.

INDEX